The Manhood of the Master

by

Harry Emerson Fosdick

Other Books from Inkling

Celebrating Middle-earth by John G. West, Jr. et al

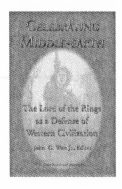

Many who read *The Lord of the Rings* notice that within the story J. R. R. Tolkien was expressing ideas about the nature of good and evil. Unfortunately, many readers lack the training to understand just what Tolkien was doing. In this book, six noted writers explain why they believe the book offers a brilliant defense of the literary, philosophical, religious and political foundations of western society as they have developed and matured.

ISBN: 1-58742-012-0 (pb) & 1-58742-013-9 (hb)

Theism and Humanism by Arthur J. Balfour

In 1962, *Christian Century* magazine asked C. S. Lewis to name the books that most influenced his thought. Among them was this book, the published version of British Prime Minister Arthur Balfour's highly popular Gifford Lectures at the University of Glasgow. Long out of print, the book that Lewis once praised as "too little read," is now available to all who are intrigued by the relationship between science and religion.

ISBN: 1-58742-005-8 (pb) & 1-58742-016-3 (hb)

Eugenics and Other Evils by G. K. Chesterton

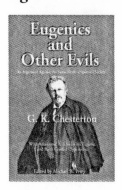

In the early decades of the twentieth century, eugenics, the scientific control of human breeding, was a popular cause within enlightened and progressive segments of Western society. Few dared to criticize it and fewer still had the courage to launch a sustained attack on what the *New York Times* praised as a wonderful "new science." Perhaps the boldest of that brave few was this talented British journalist and writer, G. K. Chesterton.

ISBN: 1-58742-002-3 (pb) & 1-58742-006-6 (hb)

These books are available online or from any bookstore (through Ingram or Baker & Taylor in the US and Bertrams in the UK). Additional details at www.InklingBooks.com

The Manhood
of the Master

The Character of Jesus Christ

by

Harry Emerson Fosdick

Pastor, First Baptist Church, Montclair, NJ
Pastor, First Presbyterian Church, New York City
Pastor, Riverside Church, New York City
Professor, Union Theological Seminary, New York City

Edited by

Michael W. Perry

Inkling Books   Seattle   2002

This edition of *The Manhood of the Master* contains the entire text of the 1913 edition of Harry Emerson Fosdick's *The Manhood of the Master,* which was copyrighted by The International Committee of Young Men's Christian Associations and published by Grosset & Dunlap of New York City (by arrangement with Association Press). The Scriptural texts are from the American Standard Version of the Revised Bible copyrighted in 1901 by Thomas Nelson and Sons. For this edition a few typographical errors in the text were corrected and minor changes were made to conform to present-day publishing standards. Also, a Foreword, pull-quotes and footnotes were added by the editor. To better indicate its subject matter, "The Character of Jesus Christ" was added as a subtitle.

Acknowledgements for this Edition

For his assistance in providing photographs of Dr. Fosdick, the editor would like to thank Victor Jordan, Associate Archivist of The Riverside Church Archives in New York City. The back cover photo was taken during Fosdick's pastorate at the First Baptist Church of Montclair, N.J. at about the time this book was written, while the other dates from the 1920s, when he lived in New York City. Some details are based on a Historical Note that is part of the Harry Emerson Fosdick Collection, at the Burke Library of Union Theological Seminary, where Dr. Fosdick taught for many years. Needless to say, the editorial remarks are my own and do not represent the views of either Riverside Church or Union Theological Seminary.

Library Cataloging Data

Fosdick, Harry Emerson (1878–1969)
The Manhood of the Master: The Character of Jesus Christ
Editor: Perry, Michael W. (1948–)
155 p. 6 x 9 inches, 152 x 229 mm, 2 graphics
BT304 .F7 2002
232 F786M
Subjects: Jesus Christ-Character, Jesus Christ-Prayer books and devotions
Keywords: Jesus Christ, Character, Christianity, Gospel
Library of Congress Control Number: 2002115315
ISBN 1-58742-017-1 (alk. paperback)
ISBN 1-58742-018-X (alk. hardback)

Inkling Books, Seattle, Washington, Internet http://www.InklingBooks.com/
Published in the United States of America on acid-free paper
First Edition, First Printing, November 2002

Contents

Foreword

As its editor, I have often wondered why I decided to bring this now ninety-year-old book back into print. Would anyone read it or was I just wasting my time? True, its author, Harry Emerson Fosdick, was one of the best known pastors of the first half of the twentieth century. For some twenty years, from 1927 to 1946, he preached to the nation on NBC radio's "National Vespers." But in a age when school children have trouble remembering what Abraham Lincoln did, Fosdick disappeared from memory long ago.

Religious conservatives have an added reason for shunning Fosdick. He is best known for a 1922 sermon entitled "Shall the Fundamentalists Win?" Fosdick's liberal bias is all over this book. The real Jesus laid great stress doing good because, whatever difficulties that might bring in this life, we will receive a hearty "well done" from God in the next. Not believing in a resurrection, Fosdick is left with far weaker motivations—that doing good feels good or that it will number us among the great souled of history.

Jesus was also unashamedly punitive. In contrast, Fosdick—as readers will discover in the second week—is almost Orwellian in his attitude toward criminals. We aren't, he tells us, to take "vengeance" on them. Instead society is to protect itself, using the "segregation of anti-social men" and "every means" to aid their "reform." That's scary stuff. Who defines anti-social? Does it include alcoholism or perhaps a desire to own guns? The first was near top of almost every anti-social list when Fosdick wrote, and the second would top that of many modern reformers. Even if the list is kept mercifully short, what about those who refuse to reform? Should society keep locked up, virtually for life, someone simply because he refuses to quit shoplifting? Finally, what sort of horrors could be included in that "all means?" Perhaps within limits being punitive isn't all that bad. At least it lets us treat people as responsible for their actions.

Interestingly, today's liberals are as likely to find Fosdick as disturbing as their conservative counterparts. For, although Fosdick's theology was liberal, his morality reflects his New England Baptist roots and was more than a little old fashioned. His was a generation that thought Christian morality could be maintained not merely without a particular orthodox theology, but almost without dogma at all.

With a theological anchor far too light to retain a grip in life's stormy sea, liberalism has drifted far from where it lay in Fosdick's youth. The response of liberal churches to the scandals of Clinton presidency illustrate that. In week three Fosdick praised a British pastor, Frederick Robertson, as a man who would, "grind his teeth and clench his fists when passing a man who he knew was bent on destroying an innocent girl." If liberals ground any teeth over Clinton's behavior with the young intern, they concealed it remarkably well. And how do you reconcile what Fosdick said (in week nine) about those who would "wrong a child" with liberal support for legalized abortion?

The fact that, whatever our beliefs, the Fosdick of long ago isn't 'one of us' is a marvelous thing. If we read only those we fully agree with, we are living pitiful lives. We need talented, stimulating writers like Fosdick to shake us out of our complacency. As G. K. Chesterton once put it: "The theory of free speech, that truth is much larger and stranger and more many-sided than we know of, that it is very much better at all costs to hear every one's account of it, is a theory that has been justified upon the whole by experiment, but which remains a very daring and even very surprising theory."

If the dogma-denying Fosdick's belief that God guided him through vague feelings causes conservative believers to question their own smug assurance of God's leading in every aspect of their lives, then that is good. It is also good if liberals begin to ask if, all too often, their churches simply add a "me too" to a world that takes no account of God.

Finally, there is the most important reason of all for reading this book. For all Fosdick's flaws, he has managed to give us a Jesus with much of the depth and complexity that we find in the Gospels.

Many conservatives have a Jesus who is far too nice, private and conformist to bear any relationship to the fiery, public, and troublesome Jesus of the Gospels. It is virtually impossible to imagine their Jesus attacking some great evil by overturning tables and chasing people about with a whip. It is even more difficult to imagine that, having done all that, he simply walks away, the temple police parting before him like so many sheep. It is clear that the Jesus of the Gospels was a man's man who inspired awe and fear, even in his enemies. In contrast, the Jesus of many conservatives seems to be a shallow and nanny-like, obsessed with making people feel good for the moment.

Liberals fare no better. Some, it is easy to suspect, see Jesus as a charismatic political figure, speaking to cheering crowds at the Democratic National Convention and supporting every fashionable liberal cause. Hardly. The real Jesus held views about divorce so strict even his pious disciples were shocked and his response to pornography was that self-mutilation was better.

With those words, I close with a hope that readers of all persuasions and points of view will find Fosdick's masterpiece about the Master both thought-provoking and life-changing.

MICHAEL W. PERRY, SEATTLE, NOVEMBER 19, 2002

The Manhood of the Master

Introduction

This book is not a life of the Master nor a study of his teaching. It is an endeavor to understand and appreciate the quality of his character. The significant events of his life are considered, but only for the sake of looking through them into the spirit of the personality who was active there. The principal emphases of his teaching are noted, but only for the sake of understanding the quality of the one from whom the teaching came.

Neither is the book an attempted contribution to the theology of the Church about Jesus. It is an endeavor, rather, to get back behind the thoughts of the centuries about him, and to see the Man Christ Jesus himself as he lives in the pages of the gospels. Such an attempt has its advantages and disadvantages. Many puzzling questions which concern the chronology of Jesus' life and the exact import of certain of his teachings, do not greatly trouble the student of his character. The broad outlines of his personality are clear and cannot be obscured by details of interpretation. Even deeper problems which concern the dates and composition of the gospels do not present a serious difficulty, for the fundamental qualities and attitudes of our Lord are to be traced in all the gospels, and this book has endeavored to confine itself to these elemental matters.

Upon the other hand, an appreciation of the Master's character, as of any other character, is necessarily subjective. It inevitably is colored by the mind in which the appreciation is made. This is true even within the gospels, for it is easy to distinguish the aspects of the Master's life and quality which each of the evangelists has stressed. Nevertheless, a sincere endeavor to appreciate the spirit and character of Jesus Christ cannot be without value to those who follow it with independent thought and reverent heart, and to such this book is offered.

Each study is divided into two sections: "Daily Readings" and "Comment for the Week." This arrangement of the book for daily devotional reading, (the "Morning Watch"), for intensive study and for Bible study group discussion, is an experiment. The Scripture selections are intended to present each week the most salient passages from the New Testament dealing with that aspect of the Master's character which is being considered. The daily comments are purposely made individual in their application; suggestive and devotional rather than informational. The weekly comments offer opportunity for a large amount of careful study, and their full value will be felt only by those who read and thoughtfully consider the Scripture references upon which the conclusions of the author have been based. It is hoped that the arrangement of the book will make its use convenient for individual devotional reading as well as for Bible study groups.

The author acknowledges his special indebtedness to Professor James Everett Frame, D. D., who with great care read the manuscript and criticised it from the viewpoint of New Testament scholarship.

Harry Emerson Fosdick

1

The Master's Joy

Daily Readings

Jesus was so joyful in his friendships and his work that he fairly was forced to defend himself, on account of it, before his enemies. The reason for Jesus' joyfulness corresponds to a universal law that the happiest people on earth are those who are doing most for others.

❖ First Day, First Week

And it came to pass, as he sat at meat in the house, behold, many publicans and sinners came and sat down with Jesus and his disciples. And when the Pharisees saw it, they said unto his disciples, Why eateth your Teacher with the publicans and sinners? But when he heard it, he said, They that are whole have no need of a physician, but they that are sick. But go ye and learn what this meaneth, I desire mercy, and not sacrifice: for I came not to call the righteous, but sinners.

Then come to him the disciples of John, saying, Why do we and the Pharisees fast oft, but thy disciples fast not? And Jesus said unto them, Can the sons of the bridechamber mourn, as long as the bridegroom is with them? but the days will come, when the bridegroom shall be taken away from them, and then will they fast.—*Matt. 9:10–15*

Have you thought of the Master largely in terms of sorrowful self-sacrifice? Then note carefully to-day's picture of him as he sits at dinner. He is plainly happy. He is with his friends and is helping people who need help, and he so rejoices in his work that he compares his disciples and himself to a bridal party on a honeymoon. Even when we turn from such a scene as this to think of the days of Jesus' persecution, we find the note of joy unquenched. "Rejoice in *that* day," he says, "and leap for joy." "The fruits of the Spirit," according to Paul, "are love, *joy*, peace." Is your life, by its radiation of real good-cheer and goodwill, bearing testimony to your friendship with the Master?

෨෧෨෧෨

❖ Second Day, First Week

And behold, they brought to him a man sick of the palsy, lying on a bed: and Jesus seeing their faith said unto the sick of the palsy, Son, be of good cheer; thy sins are forgiven.—*Matt. 9: 2*

These things have I spoken unto you, that in me ye may have peace. In the world ye have tribulation: but be of good cheer; I have overcome the world.—*John 16: 33*

And the night following the Lord stood by him, and said, Be of good cheer: for as thou hast testified concerning me at Jerusalem, so must thou bear witness also at Rome.—*Acts 23: 11*

Wherever the Master was, one of the most familiar words on his lips was, "Be of good cheer!" Consider the power *to make men happy, to win influence, to make life worth living to others,* that lies in such an attitude. Recall the proverb: "Heaviness in the heart maketh it stoop, but a good word maketh it glad." A Boston newspaper once printed this item: "The day was dark and gloomy, but Phillips Brooks walked down through Newspaper Row and all was bright." Are you commending your Christian Gospel—Gospel means *good news*—by such an attitude?

❧❧❧

❖ Third Day, First Week

And why are ye anxious concerning raiment? Consider the lilies of the field, how they grow; they toil not, neither do they spin: yet I say unto you, that even Solomon in all his glory was not arrayed like one of these.—*Matt. 6: 28, 29*

Greater love hath no man than this, that a man lay down his life for his friends. Ye are my friends, if ye do the things which I command you. No longer do I call you servants; for the servant knoweth not what his lord doeth: but I have called you friends; for all things that I heard from my Father I have made known unto you.—*John 15: 13–15*

And the third day there was a marriage in Cana of Galilee; and the mother of Jesus was there: and Jesus also was bidden, and his disciples, to the marriage.—*John 2: 1, 2*

One of the central tests of any character is the nature of its pleasures. What do you call real joy? Jesus enjoyed *nature* and *friendship* and *social life,* and so should we. Jesus loved good health, and spent much of his time healing the bodies of men. Jesus loved the *best reading* at his disposal and was perfectly at home in the prophets. All his joys were fine and high. Without going deeper into the distinctly religious sources of Jesus' joy, examine your own heart and see if you can stand the test of this question: *Where do I look for my happiness?*

ॐॐॐ

❖ Fourth Day, First Week

And he spake unto them this parable, saying, What man of you, having a hundred sheep, and having lost one of them, doth not leave the ninety and nine in the wilderness, and go after that which is lost, until he find it? And when he hath found it, he layeth it on his shoulders, rejoicing. And when he cometh home, he calleth together his friends and his neighbors, saying unto them, Rejoice with me, for I have found my sheep which was lost. I say unto you, that even so there shall be joy in heaven over one sinner that repenteth, more than over ninety and nine righteous persons, who need no repentance.

Or what woman having ten pieces of silver, if she lose one piece, doth not light a lamp, and sweep the house, and seek diligently until she find it? And when she hath found it, she calleth together her friends and neighbors, saying, Rejoice with me, for I have found the piece which I had lost. Even so, I say unto you, there is joy in the presence of the angels of God over one sinner that repenteth.—*Luke 15: 3–10*

Almost every young man or woman begins seeking joy through *getting,* and has to learn by experience that the deepest satisfaction in life lies in *serving.* Can you remember doing some real kindness for a person who had no special reason to expect it from you? Has anything in your life lingered in your memory as a much more deeply satisfactory experience? Jesus' joy was at heart this satisfaction which comes from finding lost and needy people and helping them out. This source of exhaustless delight is at every man's hand every day, and yet how many let its treasures go unclaimed!

ॐॐॐ

❖ Fifth Day, First Week

The kingdom of heaven is like unto a treasure hidden in the field; which a man found, and hid; and in his joy he goeth and selleth all that he hath, and buyeth that field.—*Matt. 13: 44*

His lord said unto him, Well done, good and faithful servant: thou hast been faithful over a few things, I will set thee over many things; enter thou into the joy of thy lord. And he also that received the two talents came and said, Lord, thou deliveredst unto me two talents: lo, I have gained other two talents. His lord said unto him, Well done, good and faithful servant: thou hast been faithful over a few things, I will set thee over many things; enter thou into the joy of thy lord.—*Matt. 25: 21–23*

---

1.   The   Master's   Joy   13

When we give up an immediate pleasure for character's sake, we are impressed with how much we have sacrificed. Jesus was impressed with how much a man had gained. Consider what you have gained by any sacrifice you ever made for character: *The approval of God through conscience, the satisfaction of overcoming your moral enemy, the greater power to conquer the next time, the approbation of those who care most for you, increased power of usefulness to others.* How much more you gained than you sacrificed! Ought not all such sacrifice to be made with joy? Nobody ever found any real, solid and permanent satisfaction in doing wrong.

෨෨෨

❖ **Sixth Day, First Week**

Blessed are the poor in spirit: for theirs is the kingdom of heaven.

Blessed are they that mourn: for they shall be comforted.

Blessed are the meek: for they shall inherit the earth.

Blessed are they that hunger and thirst after righteousness: for they shall be filled.

Blessed are the merciful: for they shall obtain mercy.

Blessed are the pure in heart: for they shall see God.

Blessed are the peacemakers: for they shall be called sons of God.

Blessed are they that have been persecuted for righteousness' sake: for theirs is the kingdom of heaven.

Blessed are ye when men shall reproach you, and persecute you, and say all manner of evil against you falsely, for my sake. Rejoice, and be exceeding glad: for great is your reward in heaven: for so persecuted they the prophets that were before you.—*Matt. 5: 3–12*

Many of our sermons, hymns and books pity Jesus because of his suffering. He spoke of his own life, even with its persecutions, as a blessed, that is, a happy life. Consider the exhaustless sources of Jesus' joy: *his trust in his Father, his boundless hope for the future, his consciousness that he had found and was doing God's will for him, his sense of God's approval on his life, and his knowledge that he was doing a great and abiding service for men.* Think of each of these in its application to your own life. May not any one of us make our lives profoundly blessed in all these ways?

෨෨෨

❖ **Seventh Day, First Week**

These things have I spoken unto you, that my joy may be in you, and that your joy may be made full.—*John 15: 11*

And ye therefore now have sorrow: but I will see you again, and your heart shall rejoice, and your joy no one taketh away from you.—*John 16: 22*

But now I come to thee; and these things I speak in the world, that they may have my joy made full in themselves.—*John 17: 13*

————

Sooner or later the circumstances of any life become adverse. Nobody wholly escapes misfortune. *Are all your joys at the mercy of things that may happen to your Have you any resources of joy that no man and no misfortune can take away from you?* Jesus had. Consider the sources of his joy mentioned yesterday, and see that they are all utterly independent of man's hostility or the adversity of circumstance. Some day every one needs such reserves of joy as Jesus had in the upper room. Are you in possession of them?

ᏱᏱᏱ

COMMENT FOR THE WEEK

The New Testament is the most joyful book in the world. It opens with joy over the birth of Jesus; and it ends with a superb picture of a multitude, which no man could number, singing Hallelujah Choruses. No matter where you open it, amid fortunate or discouraging circumstances, you always hear the note of joy. Even when a company of friends gather at a farewell supper, before their Leader is crucified, he says to them, "These things have I spoken unto you, that my joy may be in you, and that your joy may be made full" (John 15: 11). Even when their best friend has gone, the mourners take "their food with gladness, and singleness of heart, praising God" (Acts 2: 46). If they are flogged for their faith, the disciples depart from the council, rejoicing that they are "counted worthy to suffer dishonor for the Name" (Acts 5: 41); when an apostle is put in jail overnight he passes the time singing (Acts 16: 25), and if you listen to him in his Roman prison, you will hear him dictating, "Rejoice in the Lord always: again I will say, Rejoice" (Phil. 4: 4). There is enough tragedy in the New Testament to make it the saddest book in the world, and instead it is the joyfullest.

————

On the two occasions when Jesus took special pains to justify his conduct to his enemies, he was explaining to them why he and his disciples were so joyful.

————

The religion which expresses itself in this book and which issues from it, is the most joyful religion on earth. Three great missionary faiths are in existence today: Mohammedanism, Buddhism, Christianity. The first has no hymns and never sings. The second is only now endeavoring to compete with Christianity by copying our songs. Here is a specimen of Buddhist plagiarism:

O for a thousand tongues to sing
    My holy Buddha's praise:
The glories of my teacher great,
    The triumphs of his grace!

Buddha! the name that kills our fears.
    That bids our sorrows cease:
'Tis music in the speaker's ears,
    'Tis life, and health, and peace.

Hear him, ye deaf; his praise, ye dumb,
    Your loosened tongues employ;
Ye blind, behold your Buddha come;
    And leap, ye lame, for joy.

So Buddhism endeavors to graft into her pessimistic thought of life a little of that radiant hymnology in which sixty generations of Christians spontaneously have broken into song.

Behind this joyous book and this joyous religion stands a joyful personality. The mournful pictures of him in medieval art are proved to be wrong by the records of his life and the consequences of his influence. The most joyous religion and book in existence were not inspired by a melancholy man. Swinburne imagines an ancient Roman saying of him:

Thou hast conquered, O pale Galilean,
The world has grown grey with thy breath!

Was Jesus a "Pale Galilean"? Has the world "grown grey with his breath"? Let us look at him and see.

I never made a sacrifice in my life.
—David Livingstone, African Missionary

On the two occasions when Jesus took special pains to justify his conduct to his enemies, he was explaining to them why he and his disciples were so joyful. In Mark 2: 18, 19, he is justifying the refusal of his little company to fast. A Pharisee fasted twice every week, on Mondays and Thursdays, whether he felt like it or not. Jesus says that insincere, forced abstinence is useless, and that he and his disciples are as happy as a bridal party and do not wish to fast. This is a skilful way of putting the matter, because, according to the Jewish law, a bridal party was always exempt from fasting. Jesus claims that he and his friends are on a continuous honeymoon, and that the Pharisaic laws have no right to interrupt their freedom.

On another occasion the Pharisees complain because he welcomes sinners to his friendship. He tells them (Luke 15) that the work which he is doing in finding lost men and bringing them back to their true life, is the joyfullest work in the world. He says that he is as glad over it as a shepherd who calls in his neighbors for a feast when a lost sheep is rescued; as full of satisfaction as a housewife who has lost a coin and found it; as happy as a father whose prodigal son has come home. He says that this sort of experience which he is enjoying makes the angels sing, and that such joy he will not exchange for the exclusiveness of the Pharisees.

Jesus was so joyful in his *friendships* and his *work* that he fairly was forced to defend himself, on account of it, before his enemies. *The reason for Jesus' joyfulness corresponds to a universal law that the happiest people on earth are those who are doing most for others.* We say that Jesus' earthly life was the time of his humiliation and self-sacrifice, but when he speaks of it, he says in joy, "My meat is to do the will of him that sent me." He loves his life. Take him at his most disheartened day, when hostility assails him and friends desert, yet you feel that nothing could buy him off or woo him away from the work of service which he is doing. He loves it, glories in it, would be miserable if deprived of it. He finds life by losing it (Matt. 10: 39), and defines greatness in terms of usefulness (Matt. 20: 25–28). We smaller souls, when for the sake of greater good we surrender a lesser convenience, fix our thoughts and settle our remembrance on the sacrifice which we have made. But Jesus said that a man found a treasure in a field, and *in his joy sold all that he had* and bought that field (Matt. 13: 44). The emphasis of Jesus is not upon the sacrifice, but upon the joy of finding the spiritual treasure and getting it at any price. Only in great souls do you find to the full this joy in service. It is in Paul when, amid his tremendous hardships, he says, "We also rejoice in our tribulations." It is in David Livingstone, who after his terrible sufferings in Africa said, "I never made a sacrifice in my life." They felt about their work for others what Nelson felt about war, when at Aboukir, with the shot and splinters from the deck flying all about him, he said: "This is warm work and it may be the last of us at any minute," and then, as he turned away, "but I wouldn't be elsewhere for thousands!"

Another reason for this exultant spirit in Jesus is also fundamental. *He had the most joyous idea of God that ever was thought of.* He taught his disciples that they could take the most beautiful aspects of human life, like fatherhood, and lifting them up to the best they could imagine, could say, God is much better than this. "If ye then, being evil," he said, "know how to give good gifts unto your children, *how much more* shall your Father"

(Matt. 7: 11). This is the most joyous thought of God of which we know. For centuries men had enthroned in heaven their evil with their good, their jealousies, even their lusts and passions. Jesus taught men to interpret God in terms of the spiritually best they could imagine. Whatsoever things are just, true, honorable, pure, lovely, and of good report, if there was any virtue and any praise, Jesus affirmed these things of God.

When a scientist catches this method of Jesus in thinking of God, he says in the words of Sir Oliver Lodge of the University of Birmingham, "I will not believe that it is given to man to have thoughts, higher and nobler than the real truth of things." When a poet takes fire from Jesus' joyful conception of God, he pictures, as Browning does in "Saul," a man longing to help his friend, and then pictures him rising from this human love toward God to cry:

> Would I suffer for him that I love? So wouldst thou—so wilt thou!
> So shall crown thee the topmost, ineffablest, uttermost crown—
> And thy love fill infinitude wholly, nor leave up nor down
> One spot for the creature to stand in!

This thought of God is peculiarly Jesus' contribution to the world, and no other ever compared with it in joyousness. It stands to reason that no gloomy soul ever really held, much less originated such a jubilant conception of Deity.

The gospels show clearly that this joyousness of Jesus overflowed in all the familiar ways that everywhere are the signs of a radiant nature.

Out of this thought of God a boundless hope inevitably comes. Because God is unimaginably good, "exceeding abundantly above all we can ask or think," nothing is too good to be true. If three quarters of Jesus' work falls on poor ground and is lost, Jesus is sure that one quarter will come to glorious fruition (Matt. 13: 1ff). If his cause is very meager in its beginnings, he has no doubt that it will grow to a great outcome, like a mustard seed becoming a tree, or leaven fermenting the entire pan of dough (Matt. 13: 31ff). If tares and wheat are seen competing in the field of the world, Jesus never suspects that the tares will win the victory; he knows the wheat will (Matt. 13: 24–30). When his enemies grow menacing and his disciples are frightened, Jesus' hope never wavers: "Every plant which my heavenly Father planted not shall be rooted up. Let them alone" (Matt. 15: 13, 14). Jesus was perfectly sure of the victory of right over wrong. In this sense he was profoundly an optimist. It is absurd to suppose that a sad soul could hold such an undiscourageable and jubilant hope as this.

The   Manhood   of   the   Master

Give us to awaken with smiles; give us to labor smiling; and as the sun lightens the world, so let our loving-kindness make bright this house of our habitation.—Robert Louis Stevenson

The gospels show clearly that *this joyousness of Jesus overflowed in all the familiar ways that everywhere are the signs of a radiant nature.* When his enemies say that he was "a gluttonous man and a wine bibber" (Matt. 11: 19), it is a gross slander, but it is clear that such an accusation would not have gained currency, unless, like his first disciples, he had taken his food with gladness. None but a joyful soul loves children as Jesus did and finds in their artless and care-free company a solace and delight (Mark 10: 16). None but a joyful soul loves nature as Jesus did, watching the changing weather signals of an evening sky in summer (Matt. 16: 2, 3), or considering the lilies, how they grow, more beautiful than Solomon in all his glory (Matt. 6: 28, 29). None but a joyful soul could have shed over his teaching, as serious teaching as there is in the race's history, such a spontaneous play of good humor as Jesus uses. He never jests as Socrates does, but he often lets the ripple of a happy breeze play over the surface of his mighty deep. When he is teaching the disciples the necessity of patient and persistent prayer, he describes the appearance of God to the impatient man as that of a sulky neighbor in bed with his children who will not readily get up and open the door (Luke 11: 5–8). When he wishes to picture the meanness of an unforgiving spirit, he tells of a servant who had just been forgiven a debt of $12,000,000, but who went out and choked a fellow-servant who owed him $17 (Matt. 18: 23–35). When he wishes to reprove harsh judgment on the part of a man who forgets his own sins, he pictures a man with a beam in his own eye, painfully squinting to get a mote from the eye of his brother (Matt. 7: 2, 3). This reminds one of Confucius' whimsical simile: "Let every man sweep the snow from his own doors, and not trouble himself about the hoar-frost on his neighbor's tiles." When Jesus deals with people who are sick, sinful, wretched, his common exclamation is, "Be of good cheer!" Even after he has left the earth, Paul dreaming of him, hears him say, as though it were his characteristic utterance, "Be of good cheer" (Acts 23: 11). There are times when Jesus is burdened, times even when he abstains from food and gives himself to solitary prayer, but he must in all such cases have followed his own admonition to his disciples: "When ye fast, be not, as the hypocrites, of a *sad countenance:*... but thou, when thou fastest, anoint thy head, and wash thy face; that thou be not seen of men to fast" (Matt. 6: 16–18). Jesus must have been the most radiant man to be found in his day in Palestine. He must have carried with him an atmosphere of glad good-will. Like springs of fresh water by the sea, even when the salt waves of sorrow went over him, he must have come up again with inexhaustible kindliness and joy. What the gospels report once, must have been his characteristic effect on all who loved him, "Then were the disciples glad when they saw the Lord."

At first, this representation of the Master may seem to deny one of the most fundamental truths about him, *that "he was a man of sorrows and acquainted with grief."* The interpretation of Jesus' character in art and in ordinary thought has depended largely on his cries of agony: "Now is my soul troubled; and what shall I say?" (John 12: 27); "My soul is exceeding sorrowful even unto death" (Mark 14: 34). There is, however, no conflict between Jesus, "the man of sorrows," and Jesus, the man of joy. Joy and sorrow are not alien and antagonistic; they both come from the same capacity for feeling, the same breadth of sensitive surface which the soul exposes to the touch of God and of the world.

He who lives more lives than one,
More deaths than one must die.

The ocean that has sweep and depth in it for sea-going tempests, has room for calms also, with a verge and horizon to their peace that no pool can know. The place where great storms arise is the place where great calms fall. The same capacity is required by both. A man of deep sorrows and deep joys must always be the same man—with what a range and depth of feeling! Jesus is so glad in communion with his Father, that on a mountain top his very face is transfigured; and he is so broken-hearted in Gethsemane that his brow sweats blood. When he is sorrowful, no sorrow is like his; and when he is joyful, what a sweep of water and depth of sky for his gladness!

Whatever else may be true of Jesus, he was no "pale Galilean." The first impression which he makes is one of overflowing radiance and gladness.

Indeed, the impression of Jesus' joyousness is greater because of his sorrows. Jesus had been the real encourager of men because his joy sustained the shock of cruel circumstance and agonizing struggle and came off victorious. Like a rainbow, his gladness often gets part of its effect because it is built on the clouds of a preceding storm. When his trouble was at its climax in the upper room at the last supper his joy was unquenched. "Be of good cheer," he said, "I have overcome the world." The men who have most cheered their fellows are not the men of untroubled lives, but those whose spirits were too glad to be submerged by sorrow, men like Robert Louis Stevenson who, exiled to Samoa for his health, and sure to die there soon, prayed, "Give us to awaken with smiles; give us to labor smiling; and as the sun lightens the world, so let our loving-kindness make bright this house of our habitation." Such men have been the joy-bringers of the race, and Jesus is the Master of them.

Jesus' blessedness was not like a brook that flows from melting snow which can be made to vanish by the sun, but like a stream that has exhaustless springs to draw from.

This is the most significant fact about Jesus' joy, that the sources of it were not at the mercy of men and circumstance. There were sources of gladness in Jesus' life which were dependent on the good-will of men. His satisfaction in the creature-comforts of life, his delight in the free and unimpeded teaching of the people, his confidence in his disciples, including Judas—these and other doors of joy in the Master's experience, were at the mercy of men. And they closed them. All through the final months of his ministry you can hear the click of closing doors around his life, until at last they shut him into the upper room to face a terrible tomorrow. Every door which the hand of man could reach was closed. Then that wonderful thing happened, which is the mark of all exalted souls and supremely of the Master; he fell back on resources which the hand of man could not touch. "My joy I give unto you," he said, "and your joy *no man taketh from you.*" Jesus' blessedness was not like a brook that flows from melting snow which can be made to vanish by the sun, but like a stream that has exhaustless springs to draw from. He could stand anything that men or circumstances could do to him and still have resources of joy. He was an unconquerable soul. He even told his disciples that when they were persecuted, they could still "rejoice and be exceeding glad" (Matt. 5: 12).

Whatever else may be true of Jesus, he was no "pale Galilean." The first impression which he makes is one of overflowing radiance and gladness.

Notes

2

The Master's Magnanimity

When he told the story of the good Samaritan, he let us know the moral or religious state of every character in it, save one. The robbers were bad; the priest and Levite were Jews; the Samaritan was a heretic; but the victim on the road, who was he? Was he a Jew, a Gentile or a Samaritan? Was he good or bad? Was he grateful or churlish? No one knows. Jesus did not describe him save thus far, that he was a man who needed help.

Daily Readings

❖ **First Day, Second Week**

But I say unto you that hear, Love your enemies, do good to them that hate you, bless them that curse you, pray for them that despitefully use you.—*Luke 6: 27, 28*

And if ye love them that love you, what thank have ye? for even sinners love those that love them. And if ye do good to them that do good to you, what thank have ye? for even sinners do the same. And if ye lend to them of whom ye hope to receive, what thank have ye? even sinners lend to sinners, to receive again as much. But love your enemies, and do them good, and lend, never despairing; and your reward shall be great, and ye shall be sons of the Most High: for he is kind toward the unthankful and evil. Be ye merciful, even as your Father is merciful. And judge not, and ye shall not be judged: and condemn not, and ye shall not be condemned: release, and ye shall be released: give, and it shall be given unto you; good measure, pressed down, shaken together, running over, shall they give into your bosom. For with what measure ye mete it shall be measured to you again.—*Luke 6: 32–38*

Think of these words first, not as difficult commandments laid on us, but as revelations of the Master's own spirit. What a wealth of generosity! What a lavishness of goodwill! *Read the passage over, using it as a window to look into Jesus' own heart.* Remember that he both really felt and actually lived what these words express. Compare your own life now with the boundless magnanimity of the Master, and consider what it means that you cannot help being instinctively ashamed of yourself in the presence of such a spirit.

❧❧❧

❖ Second Day, Second Week

Then came Peter and said to him, Lord, how oft shall my brother sin against me, and I forgive him? until seven times? Jesus said unto him, I say not unto thee, Until seven times; but, Until seventy times seven. Therefore is the kingdom of heaven likened unto a certain king, who would make a reckoning with his servants. And when he had begun to reckon, one was brought unto him, that owed him ten thousand talents. And the lord of that servant, being moved with compassion, released him, and forgave him the debt. But that servant went out, and found one of his fellow-servants, who owed him a hundred shillings: and he laid hold on him, and took him by the throat, saying, Pay what thou owest. So his fellow-servant fell down and besought him, saying, Have patience with me, and I will pay thee. And he would not: but went and cast him into prison, till he should pay that which was due.—*Matt. 18: 21–24, 27–30*

Jesus says that an unforgiving, grudge-bearing spirit is not simply a fault, but that it is unutterably mean. Think over all that people have had to endure in you; remember the patience and forgiveness of your parents, the way your friends have overlooked your blunders and ill nature; consider how your hope of any chance to retrieve past mistakes in your moral life rests on God's mercy and willingness to pardon. Then think how mean it is to cherish grudges against those who wrong you. Face squarely all your nourished spite against any one and see how contemptible it is.

❧❧❧

❖ Third Day, Second Week

And whensoever ye stand praying, forgive, if ye have aught against any one; that your Father also who is in heaven may forgive you your trespasses.—*Mark 11: 25*

And forgive us our debts, as we also have forgiven our debtors. And bring us not into temptation, but deliver us from the evil one. For if ye forgive men their trespasses, your heavenly Father will also forgive you. But if ye forgive not men their trespasses. neither will your Father forgive your trespasses.—*Matt. 6: 12–15*

Have you ever tried to pray and found that your cherished bitterness against some unfriendly person made real praying impossible? So when the murderers of Macbeth tried to pray, "The prayer stuck in their throat." Try today to pray for the one whom you most dislike. Really desire for him the deepest good. *Pray for him so sincerely, that, in all honesty, if you had a chance to help him the next moment, you would have to do it.* Then consider yourself bound to forgive fully when the opportunity comes, to make it come now if you can, and meanwhile to let no bitterness interrupt your fellowship with God.

❧❧❧

❖ Fourth Day, Second Week

Ye have heard that it was said to them of old time, Thou shalt not kill; and whosoever shall kill shall be in danger of the judgment: but I say unto you, that every one who is angry with his brother shall be in danger of the judgment; and whosoever shall say to his brother, Raca, shall be in danger of the council; and whosoever shall say, Thou fool, shall be in danger of the hell of fire. If therefore thou art offering thy gift at the altar, and there rememberest that thy brother hath aught against thee, leave there thy gift before the altar, and go thy way, first be reconciled to thy brother, and then come and offer thy gift.—*Matt. 5: 21–24*

What does religion mean to you? Has it ever degenerated in your life into a mere observance of forms or attendance on services? Then note what Jesus says: that *true religion involves brotherliness, real, inward brotherliness, and that nothing externally religious which a man can perform means anything without that.* Of all expressions of brotherliness the most common is active, practical service; far less common is the ability to bear injuries without being vengeful, to be reviled and to revile not again, to be wronged and instead of "getting even" to help the offender. This is brotherliness in a most noble and difficult form. Are you in this sense a religious man?

❧❧❧

❖ Fifth Day, Second Week

For hereunto were ye called: because Christ also suffered for you, leaving you an example, that ye should follow his steps: who did no sin, neither was guile found in his mouth; who, when he was reviled, reviled not again; when he suffered, threatened not; but committed himself to him that judgeth righteously: who his own self bare our sins in his body upon the tree, that we, having died unto sins, might live unto righteousness; by whose stripes ye were healed.—*II Peter 2: 21–24*

And when they came unto the place which is called The skull, there they crucified him, and the malefactors, one on the right hand and the other on the left. And Jesus said, Father, forgive them; for they know not what they do.—*Luke 23: 33, 34*

———————

When we speak of unselfishness we generally mean a generous spirit of service that is willing to sacrifice. But not only do we act on other people; other people act on us; and selfishness in receiving other people's actions on us is more common than refusal to serve them. Touchiness, petulance, *supersensitiveness, readiness to have one's pride hurt and to be insulted, keeping a chip on one's shoulder, all these are forms of selfishness.* They reveal vanity, self-consciousness, a desire to be noticed and an irritable and peevish fear of being slighted. Consider the marvel of Jesus' character in this respect, as revealed in today's passages. Test your own life by it.

ह्ह्ह्

❖ Sixth Day, Second Week

And it came to pass, that he was sitting at meat in his house, and many publicans and sinners sat down with Jesus and his disciples: for there were many, and they followed him. And the scribes of the Pharisees, when they saw that he was eating with the sinners and publicans, said unto his disciples, How is it that he eateth and drinketh with publicans and sinners? And when Jesus heard it, he saith unto them, They that are whole have no need of a physician, but they that are sick: I came not to call the righteous, but sinners.—*Mark 2: 15–17*

———————

Are you not tempted to narrow your good will and brotherliness to a special clique? Is not this one of the great dangers, for example, of college life? Note that Jesus' magnanimity overpassed even the boundaries of customary propriety. *He was ready to befriend all sorts and conditions of men.* Think of your college's fraternity or sorority problem with reference to this; or of the social life in your church and community. Do you draw lines, within which you are generous, but outside of which you feel no special obligation? Is this Christian? Can anyone be a genuine disciple of the Master who consciously indulges in such social exclusiveness?

ह्ह्ह्

❖ Seventh Day, Second Week

Wherefore, putting away falsehood, speak ye truth each one with his neighbor: for we are members one of another. Be ye angry, and sin not: let not the sun go down upon your wrath: neither give place to the devil. Let him that stole steal no more: but rather let him labor, working with his hands the thing that is good, that he may have whereof to give to him that hath need. Let no corrupt speech proceed out of your mouth, but such as is good for edifying as the need may be, that it may give grace to them that hear. And grieve not the Holy Spirit of God, in whom ye were sealed unto the day of redemption. Let all bitterness, and wrath, and anger, and clamor, and railing, be put away from you, with all malice: and be ye kind one to another, tenderhearted, forgiving each other, even as God also in Christ forgave you.—*Ephesians 4: 25–32*

Whole-hearted good-will, such as is described in this passage, is the most characteristic quality of a true Christian. *One who really has it is a marked person in any company. As George Eliot said, he impresses one like a fine quotation from the Bible in the 'midst of a newspaper paragraph.* He is the best argument for Christianity on earth, far stronger than any philosophical discussion ever devised. Something like this was doubtless Daniel Webster's meaning when he said that the strongest argument for religion that he knew was an old aunt of his who lived up in the New Hampshire hills. Is anyone likely to think of our lives as a great reason for believing in Christ?

ॐॐॐ

Comment for the Week

Joy and magnanimity cannot easily exist without each other. They are naturally found together, as the fine saying of Martin Luther suggests: *"My soul is too glad and too great to be at heart the enemy of any man."* What Luther felt in his elevated moments, was the constant quality of the Master's life and teaching. His was an undiscourageable friendliness. No one's hostility could spoil his persistent good-will.

My soul is too glad and too great to be the enemy of any man.
—Martin Luther

Jesus' magnanimity is most impressively shown in his forgiveness of enemies. A large-hearted attitude toward unfriendly people was, of course, admired long before Jesus came. By men of insight it has always been regarded as a sign of moral greatness. In the Book of the Exodus, we read, "If thou meet thine enemy's ox or his ass going astray, thou shalt surely bring it back to him." When Paul in his letter to the Romans says, "If thine enemy hunger, feed him; if he thirst, give him to drink; for in so doing thou shalt heap coals of fire upon his head," he is quoting verbatim from the Book of Proverbs. In the forty-fifth chapter of Genesis, the superb scene in which Joseph forgives his brethren, we see the ancient admiration for a magnanimous man. Jesus, however, took this superlative virtue from its place as an occasional ideal, and made it the common duty of every day; he considered it an obligation, since we never can forgive as much as we have been forgiven; and he made the right attitude toward hostile men not a negative refraining from vengeance, but a positive saviorhood, that prays for them, blesses them and sacrificially seeks their good (Luke 6: 27, 28).

This overflowing good-will toward unfriendly people is one of Jesus' unique contributions to the moral life, and he was aware of the fact. When he said, "Ye have heard that it was said, An eye for an eye and a tooth for a tooth: . . . Ye have heard that it was said, Thou shalt love thy neighbor, and hate thine enemy: but I say unto you, Love your enemies" (Matt. 5: 38, 43ff), he was consciously contrasting Jewish sayings with his new commandment. When he said, "If ye salute your brethren only, what do ye more than others? do not even the Gentiles the same?" he was definitely contrasting the Graeco-Roman morals with his own. The author of "Ecce Homo" reminds us that Xenophon, one of the favorite disciples of Socrates, and a friend of Plato, in eulogizing his hero, Cyrus the Younger, climaxes his praise by saying that no one ever did more good to his friends and more harm to his enemies. Even Cicero so hated Clodius, his enemy, and was so little ashamed of it, that two years after that enemy's death at the Battle of Bovill, Cicero was dating his letters, "The 560th day after Bovill." Jesus has wrought an incalculable change in this aspect of man's life. When he came, to forgive an enemy was exceptional, a sporadic virtue not altogether admired. Today not only men who correspond to Xenophon and Cicero, but plain folk, have caught the idea that not to forgive an enemy is poor spirit—that bearing grudges is a sign of meanness.

And all is past, the sin is sinn'd, and I, Lo! I forgive thee as Eternal God forgives.—Alfred Lord Tennyson

---

Note, for example, that no ideal character can be imagined now without this Christlike quality of forgiveness. When Browning portrays the beautiful character of Pompilia in *The Ring and the Book,* the picture is not complete until Guido has wronged her cruelly, and she, with all her consciousness of the bitter injustice done her, is still steadfast in her unconquerable good will and readiness to pardon. When Tennyson imagines King Arthur, the perfect knight, the portrayal cannot be consummated until, deeply wronged by Guinevere, his Queen, he stands beside her, as she lies penitent upon the floor of the nunnery.

Thou hast not made my life so sweet to me,
That I the King should greatly care to live;
For thou hast spoilt the purpose of my life.
    * * * * *
Yet think not that I come to urge thy crimes,

I did not come to curse thee, Guinevere,
I, whose vast pity almost makes me die
To see thee, laying there thy golden head,
My pride in happier summers, at my feet.
The wrath which forced my thoughts on that fierce law,
The doom of treason and the flaming death,
(When first I learnt thee hidden here) is past.
　　　* * * * *

And all is past, the sin is sinn'd, and I,
Lo! I forgive thee, as Eternal God
Forgives.

Jesus has so impressed the world with his life and teaching of magnanimity, that no great character is now imaginable without that quality.

Note, moreover, that this attitude toward hostile people, regarded by so many as an attitude impossibly ideal, is becoming increasingly the state's attitude toward criminals. Every modern penologist has discarded the idea that the state has a right to take vengeance on a criminal. In place of the old theory that the man must be punished, "an eye for an eye," has come the new theory that society must be protected by the segregation of anti-social men, and that in that segregation every means must be used that will help in the reform of the criminal. Not vengeance on, but transformation of the malefactor is the modern principle, too recently grasped yet to have been wrought fully into our institutions. All juvenile courts, however, all systems of indeterminate sentence and parole, all reformatory methods in the prisons, mean that the state is accepting the principle of Jesus, and is growing magnanimous toward its enemies. Said Dr. Samuel J. Barrows, one of the foremost criminologists, "We speak of Howard, Livingstone, Becaria and others as great penologists who have profoundly influenced modern life; but the principles enunciated and the methods introduced by Jesus, seem to me to stamp him as the greatest penologist of any age. He has needed to wait, however, nearly twenty centuries to find his principles and methods recognized in modern law and penology."

Li Hung Chang once said that the only trouble with Jesus' ideals was that they were too lofty to be practical. He referred especially to the Master's unconquerable good will toward his enemies. Nevertheless, not only did Jesus himself live out that most elevated ideal, but *today we can neither imagine a noble character nor arrange a prison system that lacks the quality of that ideal.*

The exhibition of magnanimity which Jesus gave in his own life is one of the most wonderful revelations of his spirit. In the ancient apocryphal stories about Jesus we find tales like this:

"At another time, when Jesus was returning home with Joseph in the evening, He met a boy who ran up against Him with so much force that He fell. And Jesus said to him: As thou hast thrown me down, so thou shalt fall and not rise again. And the same hour the boy fell down and expired." We should feel the falsity of such stories, even if we did not know that they were apocryphal, for they belie all that we know about Jesus. When Samaritan villagers were inhospitable in so rough a way that the angered disciples wanted vengeance, he rebuked the spirit of his followers (Luke 9: 51–56). He knew, if ever man did, the brutality of unfriendly people. He was called a liar, a servant of the devil, a man gone mad, and a ruthlessly ambitious seeker for a worldly crown, and yet amid all this misjudgment and slander, he taught his disciples to do what he was doing—loving his enemies, doing good to those that hated him, blessing those that cursed him, praying for those that despitefully used him. Even when one of his old friends betrayed him, and was about to give him a traitor's kiss, he said: "Friend, do that for which thou art come" (Matt. 26: 50). He could not fairly use the warm word for friend which he used to his faithful disciples (*philos*), but he used a word which showed his unquenchable good will (*hetairos*). His words about forgiveness become most meaningful when we think of them as unconscious autobiographical revelations of the soul that spoke them. From them we learn that when he started to pray, he forgave from his heart all his enemies (Mark 11: 25); that when he was alone in private devotion, he was often praying for his enemies. Therefore, he was but fulfilling his life-long practice and revealing the constant quality of his spirit, when on Calvary he thought of all the unfriendly people who ever had wronged him and said, "Father, forgive them; for they know not what they do" (Luke 23: 33, 34). He is incomparably the most magnanimous soul that ever lived.

This quality in the Master becomes the more wonderful in view of the fact that *when any one holds an exalted opinion of himself and his work, he naturally resents with proportionate bitterness any disregard of his rights or interference with his plans.* So Mohammed raged against his foes, when, thinking himself the vice-regent of God, he found himself abused and his purpose thwarted. So we have seen Dowie grow hectic with anger when his claims were derided and he himself despised. 'What, then, shall we expect of one who, thinking of his truth, says, "Heaven and earth shall pass away but my words shall never pass away;" thinking of his work, says, "The Father, abiding in me, doeth his works;" thinking of himself, says, "He that hath seen me hath seen the Father"? How will he act when he is despised and rejected of men; is taken to the edge of a cliff by his old playmates to be killed (Luke 4: 28–30); is called crazy, deceitful, devilish; is betrayed, beaten, drowned with thorns, spit upon, crucified, while Barabbas, a robber, is released? That one with such an estimation of himself and his mission, subjected to such contumely and suffering, should live a life of unspoiled good-will toward all men, and when he dies should pray for the forgiveness of his enemies, is Jesus' unparalleled achievement in magnanimity. It does not come within the range of what we ordinarily mean by human nature.

One aspect of the Master's attitude toward unfriendly people is evident; *whenever a man did him a wrong, he looked upon the wrong as a sure sign of a deep need in the man's life.* An insult or a blow seemed to him a signal of moral need flung out from his enemy's heart. Jesus thought first, not of the wrong done to him, but of the pitiable need of the man who was so ignorant and perverted as to do it. When the Samaritan village used him despitefully he was sorry for the villagers rather than resentful for himself; when Judas betrayed him, he was concerned with Judas' pitiable failure-turned into an apostate when he might have been an apostle—rather than with the bitter wrong done to him. His magnanimity was simply one part of his disinterested self-forgetful love for all sorts of men. Men have many ways of revealing their need of help—by asking for it or by showing unconsciously the evidence of misery and want; but when they are bitter, unfriendly, ungrateful, they show even a deeper need. *We must think of their need and not our wrong—that is magnanimity.* It was said of Henry Ward Beecher that no one ever felt the full force of his kindness until he did Beecher an injury. This is Paul's meaning when he says, "Love taketh not account of evil" (I Cor. 13: 5); that is, does not keep a memorandum of injuries received, but forgets, forgives and tries to help.

You have more of that feeling of personal resentment than I have, perhaps I have too little of it; but I never thought it paid.
—Abraham Lincoln

Another element in Jesus' attitude toward unfriendly people is evident. *He would not allow a cherished grudge to disturb the peace of his own spirit or interrupt his communion with God.* Said Abraham Lincoln: "No man resolved to make the most of himself can spare the time for personal contention. Still less can he afford to take all the consequences, including the vitiating of his temper, and the loss of self-control. "Nothing in Lincoln's character has more charmed the admiration of his countrymen than this freedom from vindictiveness. "You have more of that feeling of personal resentment than I have," he said, on one occasion; "perhaps I have too little of it; but I never thought it paid." And once more, in words that are the revelation of an essentially magnanimous heart, he said, "I shall do nothing in malice. What I deal with is too vast for malicious dealing." Surely it is clear that as soon as we let the unfriendliness of other people arouse in us an answering bitterness, until our lives are disturbed by anger and exasperated by grudges, we have let our enemies harm us in the very citadel of our lives. Jesus never surrendered his heart to his foes. He never let his own spirit be soiled and muddied by the desire to "get even." Whatever plans of Jesus his enemies might spoil, they could not spoil him.

Jesus felt especially, that an unforgiving man could not live in fellowship with a forgiving God (Matt. 18: 21–35). If a man is completely insulated, he can safely take hold of a live wire, for electricity cannot get into a man, unless it can get out of him. So God's Spirit of good-will cannot possess a man unless it can issue from him into other lives, and a man who will not forgive cannot be forgiven (Matt. 6: 15). Therefore, Jesus said that before a man prays, he must always see that no grudges are putting his life out of tune with the fatherly God (Mark 11: 25). To be magnanimous toward his enemies was the Master's self-protection of his own soul, for vindictiveness cuts off communion with God and lays waste the spiritual life. When Booker Washington says, *"I will not let any man reduce my soul to the level of hatred,"* he is reflecting the Master's spirit. Jesus held his own life in its inward friendliness and fellowship with God above the reach of man's hostility.

I will not let any man reduce my soul to the level of hatred.
—Booker T. Washington

The magnanimity of Jesus is revealed not only in his unconquerable good-will toward his enemies, but in his brotherly love for all sorts of outcast people. The Jews of Jesus' day were narrow in their sympathies and exclusive in their social intercourse to such a degree that they were notorious for these characteristics throughout the Roman Empire, and on this account were scorned as inhumane haters of mankind by Tacitus and Juvenal. Especially in Palestine the Jews looked upon all Gentiles as ceremonially unclean and as outside the compass of God's favor. No Jew would enter a Gentile's house or eat with him, and when Gamaliel taught that a Jew should give the customary salutation, "Peace be with you," to a Gentile, even on a pagan festal day, and that the Gentile poor should have equal rights with the Jewish poor in gleaning after harvest, he was looked upon as dangerously liberal. If Gamaliel was liberal in these slight allowances of a humane spirit, the exclusiveness of the Jew in its worst forms found expression in prayers like this: "O Lord, thou hast said that for our sakes thou madest this world. As for the other nations, which also come of Adam, thou hast said that they are nothing, and are like unto spittle—and thou hast likened the abundance of them unto a drop that falleth from a vessel" (II Esdras 6: 55, 56).

To be sure, a history worthy of admiration lay behind this Jewish illiberality. The Jews, by their exclusiveness, had saved their national existence. At their best they were illiberal, not from a mean spirit, but from an intense devotion to their Law, and from a willingness at all costs to keep themselves free from the pollution of men who neither believed nor kept the Law; and in many crises, such as accompanied the Maccabaean wars, they had proved their passionate earnestness in protecting their religious life from Gentile defilement. In spite, however, of the worthy motive which lay behind the narrowness of Jewish sympathies, it was impossible for such boundaries to circumscribe the good will of the Master. His brotherliness overflowed all the customary confines of fraternity. Publicans were hated by the Jews as traitors to their race. "Their money was tainted money; it would not be accepted in the synagogue. Their oath was absolutely worthless; they could not be witnesses in any court of law. If a man promised to do a thing for a publican under oath, he was not bound to keeps his pledge." Jesus overleaped in his compassion this Jewish antipathy, and welcomed publicans to his discipleship (Matt. 9: 10–13). Samaritans were the object of an inherited Jewish grudge, and a strict Pharisee would not even walk in Samaritan territory for fear of being made unclean. Jesus admired Samaritans (Luke 10: 33–37); and did his best to help them (John 4: 7–10). As for the Gentiles he took them into his care and hope, and while counting himself sent first to Israel (Matt. 10: 5, 6; Matt. 15: 22ff), he said that the nations would come from the east and west, from north and south, and sit down with Abraham, Isaac and Jacob in the Kingdom (Matt. 8: 11). He was too great to be bound by Jewish exclusiveness. Nothing human was alien from his love. When he told the story of the good Samaritan, he let us know the moral or religious state of every character in it, save one. The robbers were bad; the priest and Levite were Jews; the Samaritan was a heretic; but the victim on the road, who was he? Was he a Jew, a Gentile or a Samaritan? Was he good or bad? Was he grateful or churlish? No one knows. Jesus did not describe him save thus far, that he was *a man who needed help.* Wherever humanity was in want, no matter what the creed or race or character, there Jesus' good-will sought a chance to serve. Such is the magnanimity of Jesus and it ushered in a new era in human brotherhood.

A soul, radiant with joy that no circumstances could quench, overflowing with generosity that no injuries could embitter and no antipathies could narrow, such is the impression of the Master's manhood.

෨෬෬

3

The Master's Indignation

Think frankly and fearlessly of the vices, meannesses, dishonesties, hypocrisies in the life about you, in the presence of which Jesus would be indignant. Where do you stand with reference to them? Are you guilty? If not, are you complacent in the presence of them, or whenever a fitting and useful chance comes, do you let your scorn of them be felt? Are you yourself living a life that makes such scorn effective?

Daily Readings

❖ First Day, Third Week

And he entered again into the synagogue; and there was a man there who had his hand withered. And they watched him, whether he would heal him on the sabbath day; that they might accuse him. And he saith unto the man that had his hand withered, Stand forth. And he saith unto them, Is it lawful on the sabbath day to do good, or to do harm? to save a life, or to kill? But they held their peace. And when he had looked round about on them with anger, being grieved at the hardening of their heart, he saith unto the man, Stretch forth thy hand. And he stretched it forth; and his hand was restored. And the Pharisees went out, and straightway with the Herodians took counsel against him, how they might destroy him.— *Mark 3: 1–6*

Pictures of Jesus, with a wan, sad face, and sermons emphasizing his meekness and humility, have left the widespread impression that quiet peacefulness was the dominant quality of the Master. *Consider this passage, then, and see how intensely indignant he could be and how his wrath could dare the hostility of men who had power to kill him.* Is not wrath a part of every great character's equipment? Consider the Psalmist's outburst:

Hot indignation hath taken hold upon me,
Because of the wicked that forsake Thy law.
I hate every false way.
I hate them that are of a double mind;
I hate and abhor falsehood.

Think over the times in your life when you were angry. Did your anger have the quality of Jesus' indignation?

ॐ ॐ ॐ

❖ Second Day, Third Week

It were well for him if a millstone were hanged about his neck, and he were thrown into the sea, rather than that he should cause one of these little ones to stumble.—*Luke 17: 2*

And in the hearing of all the people he said unto his disciples, Beware of the scribes, who desire to walk in long robes, and love salutations in the marketplaces, and chief seats in the synagogues, and chief places at feasts; who devour widows' houses, and for a pretense make long prayers: these shall receive greater condemnation.—*Luke 20: 45–47*

Why are we so often ashamed of our outbursts of anger? Would the Master ever have to regret his indignation over little children wronged or widows robbed by oily hypocrites? One of Frederick W. Robertson's friends said: "I have seen him grind his teeth and clench his fists when passing a man who he knew was bent on destroying an innocent girl."[1] Will such anger ever call for remorse? *Is not our anger generally personal resentment because of some private wrong! Is not that the reason why we are so often ashamed of our outbursts? Our wrath is altogether selfish.* Consider then that the Master never spoke a word of anger when they brutally mistreated *him;* his indignation was aroused only over the abuse of *others.* What does Paul mean by, "Be ye angry and sin not"?

**I have seen him grind his teeth and clench his fists when passing a man who he know was bent on destroying an innocent girl.
—A friend of Frederick W. Robertson**

ॐ ॐ ॐ

❖ Third Day, Third Week

Woe unto you, scribes and Pharisees, hypocrites! for ye tithe mint and anise and cummin, and have left undone the weightier matters of the law,

1. Editor: Frederick W. Robertson (1816–53) was a gifted preacher in Brighton, England. Troubled by painful illness, he died at the age of 37. He once remarked, "I go into the country to feel God; dabble in chemistry to feel awe of Him; read the life of Christ, to understand, love, and adore Him. . . . I turn with disgust from everything to Christ."

justice, and mercy, and faith: but these ye ought to have done, and not to have left the other undone. Ye blind guides, that strain out the gnat, and swallow the camel!

Woe unto you, scribes and Pharisees, hypocrites! for ye cleanse the outside of the cup and of the platter, but within they are full from extortion and excess. Thou blind Pharisee, cleanse first the inside of the cup and of the platter, that the outside thereof may become clean also.

Woe unto you, scribes and Pharisees, hypocrites! for ye are like unto whited sepulchres, which outwardly appear beautiful, but inwardly are full of dead men's bones, and of all uncleanness. Even so ye also outwardly appear righteous unto men, but inwardly ye are full of hypocrisy and iniquity.—*Matt. 23: 23–28*

Plainly when the Master spoke these words he was thoroughly indignant. Supposing that he were to come to your university or community, is there anything in the social life at which his indignation would rise? *Think frankly and fearlessly of the vices, meannesses, dishonesties, hypocrisies in the life about you, in the presence of which Jesus would be indignant.* Where do you stand with reference to them? Are you guilty? If not, are you complacent in the presence of them, or whenever a fitting and useful chance comes, do you let your scorn of them be felt? Are you yourself living a life that makes such scorn effective?

❧❧❧

❖ Fourth Day, Third Week

Now there was a certain rich man, and he was clothed in purple and fine linen, faring sumptuously every day: and a certain beggar named Lazarus was laid at his gate, full of sores, and desiring to be fed with the crumbs that fell from the rich man's table; yea, even the dogs came and licked his sores. And it came to pass, that the beggar died, and that he was carried away by the angels into Abraham's bosom: and the rich man also died, and was buried. And in Hades he lifted up his eyes, being in torments.—*Luke 16: 19–23*

Jesus is plainly indignant at the selfishness of Dives. What excuse do you think Dives made for himself? Perhaps he said that because he had not caused Lazarus' poverty, he was not *responsible* for it. Is that a good excuse? *If a man sees a fire, and does not give the alarm, is he not a partner with the man who started it?* When the priest and Levite go by on the other side and do not help, Jesus considers them partners with the robbers who did the damage! Are you doing all that you can to make the moral life of your community its best? Can you evade responsibility because you do not actively cause the evil?' Consider what you can do to help.

> **Let it be said with distinctness that love like that of the Master is terrible. It looks on Lazarus—*and then it looks on Dives!* It looks on the little children in the factory—and then on the men who profit by their labor and on the society that allows the outrage. It looks on the poor struggling for bread—and then on the men who keep food prices artificially high. It looks on the "abandoned girl"—and then on the man who betrayed her and on the men who seek pleasure at the cost of her shame.**

❧❧❧

❖ Fifth Day, Third Week

And the Passover of the Jews was at hand, and Jesus went up to Jerusalem. And he found in the temple those that sold oxen and sheep and doves, and the changers of money sitting: and he made a scourge of cords, and cast all out of the temple, both the sheep and the oxen; and he poured out the changers' money, and overthrew their tables; and to them that sold the doves he said, Take these things hence; make not my Father's house a house of merchandise His disciples remembered that it was written, Zeal for thy house shall eat me up.—*John 2: 13–17*

Consider Jesus' wrath at a great public evil, a system of legalized graft housed in God's temple. What would be his attitude today towards the corruption of our city governments and the spoiling of our democracy by graft? Is not all sincere work for civic purity real devotion to the Father's business? *Consider your plan for your life work and see whether the motive of your choice is indignation at the evils that are ruining men, and determination to bear a hand in abolishing them.* Cannot a man serve this Cause in any profession? In business? In the home-life?

❧❧❧

❖ Sixth Day, Third Week

Judge not, that ye be not judged. For with what judgment ye judge, ye shall be judged: and with what measure ye mete, it shall be measured unto you. And why beholdest thou the mote that is in thy brother's eye, but considerest not the beam that is in thine own eye? Or how wilt thou say to thy brother, Let me cast out the mote out of thine eye; and lo, the beam is in thine own eye? Thou hypocrite, cast out first the beam out of thine own eye; and then shalt thou see clearly to cast out the mote out of thy brother's eye.—*Matt. 7: 1–5*

How do you reconcile Jesus' severe condemnations with these injunctions to judge leniently? *Consider today how easy it is to condemn others. May not a man be tempted to let even righteous indignation run away with him?* Why is Jesus' wrath so tremendously impressive? Is it not because he loved men, and tried to see all the good he could discover in them, before he condemned their evil? Are you harsh, bitter, acrid in your criticism? Consider that your scorn of evil will never do any good unless your fellows feel that you judge yourself as severely as you do them, and that you appreciate their good as well as hate their evil.

ॐॐॐ

❖ Seventh Day, Third Week

Again, the devil taketh him unto an exceeding high mountain, and showeth him all the kingdoms of the world, and the glory of them; and he said unto him, All these things will I give thee, if thou wilt fall down and worship me. Then saith Jesus unto him, Get thee hence, Satan: for it is written, Thou shalt worship the Lord thy God, and him only shalt thou serve. Then the devil leaveth him.—*Matt. 4: 8–11*

And he began to teach them, that the Son of man must suffer many things, and be rejected by the elders, and the chief priests, and the scribes, and be killed, and after three days rise again. And he spake the saying openly. And Peter took him, and began to rebuke him. But he turning about, and seeing his disciples, rebuked Peter, and saith, Get thee behind me, Satan; for thou mindest not the things of God, but the things of men.—*Mark 8: 31–33*

Note that Jesus did not take a mild attitude toward evil suggestions that arose to tempt him. He hated them. He abhorred evil. *No man is safe until he learns not to dally with temptation but to repel it immediately and instinctively with fierce indignation.* Think over your besetting temptations. What suggestions of evil most endanger your character? Are you accustomed to repel them with determined abhorrence, such as rings in the Master's words, "Get thee behind me, Satan"?

ॐॐॐ

Comment for the Week

At first sight anger seems to be the opposite of a boundless good will. If it really is, then what we have said about Jesus' magnanimity is not all true. Jesus in a synagogue meeting where the elders were more anxious to have their law observed than to have a sick man healed, looked round on them with blazing anger (Mark 3: 5); he faced the organized grafting system in the temple courts, and actually used a whip of cords as he indignantly drove out the money changers (John 2 13–17); and from the hypocrisy of the Pharisees he shrank with so turbulent an indignation that words are strained in carrying the weight of his resentment. How shall we reconcile what we have said about the Master's boundless good will with these outbursts of tremendous wrath?

It may be said in general that *all great virtues are the results of two moral forces pulling in opposite directions,* just as the equilibrium of the earth is the result of centripetal and centrifugal gravitation. Liberality, for example, is merely weak and unintelligent toleration, unless with broad sympathies upon the one side there are positive convictions about truth upon the other. Conviction without sympathy makes the bigot; sympathy without conviction makes the sentimentalist; together they make the truly liberal man. So love degenerates into a vague diffusion of kindly feeling unless it is balanced by the capacity for righteous indignation. Without the abhorrence of evil, kindness becomes undiscriminating and flaccid; without kindness the abhorrence of evil becomes bitter and hateful; together, they make the magnanimous man, who, by as much as he loves his fellows, by so much hates the evils that destroy them.

Without the abhorrence of evil, kindness becomes undiscriminating and flaccid; without kindness the abhorrence of evil becomes bitter and hateful.

How weak a thing good will may become if not coupled with righteous indignation may be seen today in India. The great Indian religions preach love and good-will. A typical Buddhist saint for years has been immured within the walls of the sacred city of Benares. He sits in seclusion contemplating the Infinite and feeling benign good-will toward all creation. No grudge is allowed to disturb his kindly equanimity. He loves all men, good and evil, learned and ignorant, and no grit of hatefulness impedes the smooth running of his meditation. But he never lifts a finger to help a person, nor feels a stir of indignation at the evils of his land. When a typical Christian comes, however, love and good will mean to him a different thing. They involve positive abhorrence. He hates the system that makes debauchery with nautch girls[2] an act of religious worship; he resents the apathy that leaves millions without education; he cannot endure the traditions which enslave child-widows; he is turbulent with anger at the spectacle of famine sufferers unaided by wealthy neighbors. *A good Christian is a man of wrath, whether in India or in America.* He has heard the injunction of Paul who writes the thirteenth chapter of I Corinthians on love, and then says, "Ye that love the Lord hate evil."

2. Editor: In India "nautch girls" are a type of professional dancer.

This attitude of the Christian is a direct inheritance from Jesus. *His wrath is the negative electricity at one end of his life, caused by the positive electricity of his love at the other end, and by a law of eternal necessity the two are equal.* Because he pities the unfortunate, his indignation is profound when he sees a Pharisee robbing widows of their property and for a pretense making long prayers (Mark 12: 40). Because he cannot abide insincerity, he looks in speechless wrath on a group of men, who, themselves guilty of immoral practices, are, on the basis of the "double standard," one for women and another for men, condemning a pitiable victim of man's lust (John 8: 3–11). Because he loves all mankind, his anger is kindled at the sight of a selfish Dives who can enjoy his luxury at ease while Lazarus in distress lies at his very door (Luke 16: 19–31). In the presence of the scribes and Pharisees, who regard the smallest ceremonial demanded by the Law as God's requirement along side of "justice and mercy and faith," he is so roused in spirit that, as Dr. Seeley says: "Of the teachers of the past whose sayings have been preserved, Mohammed would be regarded by most as the type of unrelenting severity, and yet we may search the Koran from beginning to end, without finding words expressive of more vehement condemnation than those attributed to Christ" (see Matt. 23).

Let it be said with distinctness that love like that of the Master is terrible. It looks on Lazarus—*and then it looks on Dives!* It looks on the little children in the factory—and then on the men who profit by their labor and on the society that allows the outrage. It looks on the poor struggling for bread—and then on the men who keep food prices artificially high. It looks on the "abandoned girl"—and then on the man who betrayed her and on the men who seek pleasure at the cost of her shame. It looks on the unprivileged, coming to their graves, as Sydney Smith said, "with soul scarred like a soldier's body"—and then on the privileged who have enjoyed their fat feasts of opportunity within sight of the starving and have not helped. A feeble and negative benignity can observe these wrongs to men and be unstirred, but a positive love, like the Master's, is roused from its depths with indignation. His words flame up with that scathing power which profound passion alone can give. We do well to praise the love of Christ, but we do well also to remember that a man might better call on the mountains to cover him than to stand naked and defenceless before the indignation which that love creates.

One distinguishing mark of this indignation of Jesus is that he never is angry at any wrong done to him as an individual. His indignation is always unselfish. He has within him capacities for wrath much greater than ours, as the sea has room for tides which pools cannot know. Stephen H. Tyng was once rebuked by a young minister for losing his temper, and he replied,

"Young man, I control more temper every fifteen minutes than you will in a lifetime." Jesus had a capacious moral indignation, with the like of which we never shall have to deal, and yet when they spat upon him, mocked him, scourged him, crucified him, he did not resent by an angry word all the public brutality to which he was subjected. "Who, when he was reviled, reviled not again; when he suffered, threatened not" (I Peter 2: 23). He never was angry at a private wrong. "Whosoever shall speak a word against the Son of man, it shall be forgiven him," he said (Matt. 12: 32). This freedom from all personal resentment on the part of one so capable of indignation far surpasses all that we can imagine of ordinary human nature. In the light of this incomparable spirit of the Master, one can easily feel the meaning of George Matheson's confession, *"There are times when I do well to be angry, but I have mistaken the times."*

The truth of Christ's teaching seems to be this: in our own person and fortune, we should be ready to accept and pardon all; it is our cheek we are to turn; it is our coat we are to give away to the man who has taken our cloak. But when another's face is buffeted perhaps a little of the lion will become us best. That we are to suffer others to be injured and stand by, is not conceivable and surely not desirable.—Robert Louis Stevenson

---

Let anyone, however, harm another and Jesus is profoundly stirred. They used to punish criminals in that day by drowning them in Galilee with stones around their neck. Jesus says a man would be better to have that happen to him than to wrong "one of these little ones" (Luke 17: 2). Annas, the high-priest, had built up a thoroughly articulated system of graft in Jerusalem. For one thing all Jews were compelled to change their own money into special Temple currency before they could buy sacrificial beasts or pay their tithes. There was a rake-off on all this exchange and it went to the authorized money-changers and to their employers. Moreover no beast could be offered in sacrifice until it was passed upon by official examiners, and these examiners could easily refuse animals not bought from the official dealers in the Temple courts. It was a well-worked system of graft. The authorities were trading on the piety of the people. The Temple was literally a "den of thieves." When Jesus faced this situation, his indignation overflowed, and in a dramatic protest against the evil and a challenge to the "system," he drove the traders out (John 2: 13–16). Herod, a man despicable in private life and oppressive in his rule, is mentioned in Jesus' presence, and the Master's feeling is indignantly expressed: "Go and say to that fox" (Luke 13: 32). Whenever Jesus' wrath appears it always concerns a wrong done to others, a public evil that needs redress, but it never concerns a private injury. Robert Louis Stevenson has summed up the matter well: "The truth of Christ's teaching seems to be this: in our own person and fortune, we should be ready to accept and pardon all; it is our cheek we are to turn; it is our coat we are to give away to the man who has taken our cloak. But when another's face is buffeted perhaps a little of the lion will become us best. That we are to suffer others to be injured and stand by, is not conceivable and surely not desirable."

The full meaning of Jesus' indignation and the marvellous restraint with which he used it can be understood only when we *contrast the wrath of Jesus with his appreciation of any good discoverable anywhere in men.* Condemnation is negative. By itself alone it accomplishes nothing. This is clearly so in personal relationships. Granted that with incisive judgment and scathing word you have condemned a neighbor's sin, blue penciling him all over like the examination paper of a poor scholar: if that is the summation of your attitude, you have not helped him. Perhaps he knew better than you did where he was failing. Perhaps he could take up the blue pencil where you laid it down, and could go on, saying about inward matters that you could not touch, "Wrong here!" Very likely he has often stood before his life like the painter of Sienna before his canvas, saying, "God pity me that I do not do it better!" Condemnation, by itself, is alike unjust and injurious. It often merely confirms a man's discouraged opinion of himself and hardens him against all further appeals from his critic.

It is necessary, therefore, to see Jesus' righteous indignation balanced by his eager desire to discover and applaud even the faint beginnings of goodness in any man. *Jesus was the most appreciative spirit that ever lived.* He saw in Peter, the vacillating and impetuous, possibilities that Peter never dreamed of in himself. He sat in the Temple treasury and watched the Jewish men of wealth give ostentatiously out of their surplus, while a poor widow, half-ashamed of her insignificant offering, half-defiant because it was the very best that she could do, stole among them and deposited her two mites. And Jesus, deeply touched by her devotion, praised her: "This poor widow cast in more than all they that are casting into the treasury" (Mark 12: 41–44). When Mary "wasted money," as any practical man would say, by expending an extravagant sum on an ointment with which to express her boundless gratitude, Jesus so appreciated the motive behind the act that he would not allow her to be upbraided. "Let her alone," he said, "she hath done what she could" (Mark 14: 3–9). He was so appreciative of all attempts at service that he said not even a cup of cold water would go unrewarded (Matt. 10: 42); that if a man had only two talents and used them well he would be praised as much as one who served with ten talents (Matt. 25: 14, 23); that folks who are kind to the sick, imprisoned, naked, hungry, would have their ministry remembered in the judgment even though it was so small that they had quite forgotten it (Matt. 25: 37–40). He appreciated even young men who were not earnest enough to follow him (Mark 10: 17-22); he made excuses for his disciples even when they would not watch with him (Matt. 26: 36–41); and he attributed to ignorance the enmity of those who crucified him (Luke 23: 34). He had hopes of even the most abandoned (Luke 15: 11ff) and a man had only to begin to be sorry for his sin before Jesus was radiant with hope and good cheer (Luke 19: 8, 9). Whenever he saw any first sign of penitence, any small sprouting of goodness, he rose upon it with the sun of his praise, he rained on it with his glad encouragement. As he himself put it, while the *prodigal son was yet a great way off,* he ran and fell on his neck and kissed him (Luke 15: 20). Dr. Robinson has preserved for us an old Persian legend, which illustrates this aspect of the Master's character: "According to the legend, Jesus arrived one evening at the gates of a certain city and sent His disciples forward to prepare supper, while He himself, intent on doing good, walked through the streets into the market-place. He saw at the corner of it some people gathered together, looking at an object on the ground, and He drew near to see what it might be. It proved to be a dead dog, with a halter around its neck, by which it appeared to have been dragged through the dirt, and a viler, a more abject, a more unclean thing, never met the eyes of man. 'Faugh,' said one, stopping his nose, 'it pollutes the air.' 'How long,' said another, 'shall this foul beast offend our sight?' 'Look at his torn hide,' said a third, 'one could not even cut a shoe out of it.' 'And his ears,' said a fourth, 'all draggled and bleeding.' 'No doubt,' said a fifth, 'he has been hanged for thieving.' And Jesus heard them, and looking down compassionately on the dead creature, He said, 'Pearls cannot equal the whiteness of his teeth.' And the people turned towards Him in amazement, and said among themselves, 'Who is this? This must be Jesus of Nazareth, for who else could find anything to pity or approve in a dead dog?' And being ashamed they bowed their heads before Him, and went on their way."

He can rebuke Peter sharply, and Peter will love him all the better for it, because Peter knows that the Master appreciated the flowers in his life before he condemned the weeds.

Only in the light of this appreciativeness of Jesus can we understand why he has been the great encourager of men. Without it the Master would be the most discouraging person in history. He is so spotlessly perfect, "in the white light that beats upon a throne;" he is so lofty in his requirements, demanding not outward deed alone but inward quality; and he is so vehement in his condemnation of all insincerity, selfishness and pride, that he might well discourage us. But his deep and beautiful appreciation of all that is even beginning to be right in a man's life; his taking of the will for the deed, when the will is earnest; his insight to perceive possibilities of a new life where others have no hope—these things make him the great encourager of men. He judges men not simply on the basis of what they *possess,* or of what they *do,* or even of what they *are*—but on the basis of what they *may become,* and he endeavors to bring out the best in men by appreciating it, by saying now what he knows God longs to say in the end, "Well done!"

This appreciativeness of Jesus is the quality which makes his indignation so effective. One always feels that he has sought diligently for something in a man to love, before ever he lets loose on him his condemnation. He can rebuke Peter sharply (Mark 8: 31-33), and Peter will love him all the better for it, because Peter knows that the Master appreciated the flowers in his life before he condemned the weeds. Jesus' wrath is turned only against wickedness that is proud, impenitent and unrelenting. He scourges the cruel who rob widows and enjoy the profits; the hypocrites who use pious practices as a covering for their self-indulgence; the proud who thank God that they are not as other men are; the corrupt who make unjust gain out of the Temple services. Yet one feels that at the first sign of repentance Jesus' wrath would melt into tenderness and the desire to help. Indeed the twenty-third chapter of Matthew, the most terrible outburst of the Master's wrath, ends with the most wonderful overflow of his love to be found in any one verse of the gospels: "O Jerusalem, Jerusalem, that killeth the prophets, and stoneth them that are sent unto her! how often would I have gathered thy children together, even as a hen gathereth her chickens under her wings, and ye would not!" So like a terrific storm ending in a rainbow, Jesus' wrath comes to its close in love. Or if we take the setting given by Luke to this compassionate outburst of the Master, there too it comes as the consummation of indignant rebuke against evil (Luke 13: 31–34). The Master's magnanimity is made far more meaningful because he could be so deeply indignant; and his indignation is far more searching because it came from such a friendly and appreciative heart.

Here, then, are the marks of Jesus' indignation. He hated evil tremendously because he loved the people whom evil was ruining; his wrath always was unselfish, he never was angry at a private wrong; and his indignation always followed his attempt to find something praiseworthy in a man's life and was always ready to cease when the first sign of penitence appeared. Wrath like this explains the exclamation of a wise Englishman:

"Anger is one of the sinews of the soul; he who lacks it hath a maimed mind."

Notes

The   Manhood   of   the   Master

4

The Master's Loyalty to His Cause

We are therefore like soldiers doing battle under a great general. We do not know all his plans but we trust him. We do not even understand all the supernal diplomacy that has made this war here necessary; that is the general's affair, not ours. Our business is to fight under orders and help make every generation's battle another skirmish won in God's campaign.

Daily Readings

❖ **First Day, Fourth Week**

Not every one that saith unto me, Lord, Lord, shall enter into the kingdom of heaven; but he that doeth the will of my Father who is in heaven. Many will say to me in that day, Lord, Lord, did we not prophesy by thy name, and by thy name cast out demons, and by thy name do many mighty works? And then will I profess unto them, I never knew you: depart from me, ye that work iniquity.

Every one therefore that heareth these words of mine, and doeth them, shall be likened unto a wise man, who built his house upon the rock: and the rain descended, and the floods came, and the winds blew, and beat upon that house; and it fell not: for it was founded upon the rock.—*Matt. 7: 21–25*

Have you ever thought of the Master as being subtly pleased and flattered by all the people who call him, "Lord"? Think how unworthy this would be in any one and how impossible it is in him. *Would any university professor be worthy of the name if he accepted personal compliments in the place of hard work on his courses?* Consider your own Christian life in the light of today's searching passage. Some one has said that to call Jesus, "Lord" is orthodoxy; to call him, "Lord, Lord," is piety; but that neither one nor both of them can satisfy him, unless accompanied by real devotion to his Cause.

ஒ᠆ஒ᠆ஒ

❖ Second Day, Fourth Week

And one said unto him, Behold, thy mother and thy brethren stand without, seeking to speak to thee. But he answered and said unto him that told him, Who is my mother? and who are my brethren? And he stretched forth his hand towards his disciples, and said, Behold, my mother and my brethren! For whosoever shall do the will of my Father who is in heaven, he is my brother, and sister, and mother.—*Matt. 12: 47–50*

Jesus says here that only those who do God's will for them can belong to his family. You believe that God has a will in general; have you ever faced seriously the fact that he must have a plan especially for your life? *There can be no real plan for the whole that does not include a plan for all the parts; there can be no will of God for the whole world that does not include a will for your life.* Some men, like captains of ocean liners, know that there is a course marked out particularly for them and they are trying not to miss it; some, like pleasure sailors out for fun, go any way as chance caprice suggests. Which sort of life are you leading?

ஒ᠆ஒ᠆ஒ

❖ Third Day, Fourth Week

In the meanwhile the disciples prayed him, saying, Rabbi, eat. But he said unto them, I have meat to eat that ye know not. The disciples therefore said one to another, Hath any man brought him aught to eat? Jesus saith unto them, My meat is to do the will of him that sent me, and to accomplish his work.—*John 4: 31–34*

If any man willeth to do his will, he shall know of the teaching. —*John 7: 17*

Have you entered at all into the spirit of Jesus as he seeks continually to know and do what God wills for him? Consider how a man may discover just what God wants with his life. *He must be willing to do whatever God wills for him; he must be loyal to as much of God's will as he knows; he must ask habitually, not once in a while, "What wilt thou have me to do?"; he must test all his choices by the principles of Jesus; he must tune his conscience and his intelligence by prayer until God can speak through them.* Does this describe your life?

ஒ᠆ஒ᠆ஒ

❖ Fourth Day, Fourth Week

From that time began Jesus to preach, and to say, Repent ye; for the kingdom of heaven is at hand.

And Jesus went about in all Galilee, teaching in their synagogues, and preaching the gospel of the kingdom.—*Matt. 4:17, 23*

After this manner therefore pray ye: Our Father who art in heaven, Hallowed be thy name. Thy kingdom come. Thy will be done, as in heaven, so on earth.—*Matt. 6: 9–10*

Consider the Master as a patriot for a great Cause. Is not this sort of loyalty an element in all noble characters? Think of Livingstone, Luther, Florence Nightingale, Lincoln. No character was ever counted great without loyalty to a cause, without standing for something more than himself. *The Kingdom of God on earth, the rule of righteousness in the personal life and social relationships of all mankind was Jesus' Cause.* Consider how he lived for it, prayed for it, suffered for it, died for it. Are you really a patriot for the Cause of the Master? Can he rely on you at all costs to be loyal?

Jesus was not a Hegel, philosophizing unmoved within sound of the guns of Jena; he was a Leader planning the transformation of the world, and calling men to be patriots for his Kingdom. "I came to cast fire upon the earth," he said, "and what do I desire if it is already kindled?" "Think not that I came to send peace on the earth: I came not to send peace, but a sword"

ಎಲ್ಲೆಲ್ಲ

❖ Fifth Day, Fourth Week

Ye are the salt of the earth: but if the salt have lost its savor, wherewith shall it be salted? it is thenceforth good for nothing, but to be cast out and trodden under foot of men. Ye are the light of the world. A city set on a hill cannot be hid. Neither do men light a lamp, and put it under the bushel, but on the stand; and it shineth unto all that are in the house. Even so let your light shine before men; that they may see your good works, and glorify your Father who is in heaven.—*Matt. 5: 13–16*

Jesus says here that his disciples are more than mere individuals. They represent his Cause, they stand for him in the world; his honor, reputation, success are in their hands. Consider how true it is that every man has a power to represent something more than himself, and that he always comes to stand for a type of character or a special human interest in the minds of his acquaintances. Can you think of Beethoven without thinking of music? Can you think of Wm. Lloyd Garrison without thinking of the abolition of slavery? Can you think of Jesus without thinking of the cause of God and righteousness in the world? *What do your fellows think of when you come to their minds? What is the reference of your life? For what do you stand in your university or community?*

❧❧❧

❖ Sixth Day, Fourth Week

No man can serve two masters: for either he will hate the one, and love the other; or else he will hold to one and despise the other. Ye cannot serve God and mammon.—*Matt. 6: 24*

He that is not with me is against me; and he that gathereth not with me scattereth.—*Matt. 12: 30*

But seek ye first his kingdom, and his righteousness; and all these things shall be added unto you.—*Matt. 6: 33*

Face in your own life today the serious fact that you always stand for God's cause or the opposite, and that in the long run no one ever succeeds in standing for both. When a man sins he becomes a representative, an ambassador, an ally of the forces of destruction in human life. Consider the terrible effects of sensual vice on the race. Then think what it means that any one who indulges in vice is a representative of that cause. Is not the same true of gambling? dishonesty? lying? *Sin is treachery to the cause of human welfare; it is going over to the race's enemies in the spirit of Benedict Arnold. Righteousness is loyalty to the Cause of the world's salvation. In the long run you cannot be on both sides. Which are you standing for!*

❧❧❧

❖ Seventh Day, Fourth Week

Then cometh Jesus with them unto a place called Gethsemane, and saith unto his disciples, Sit ye here, while I go yonder and pray. And he took with him Peter and the two sons of Zebedee, and began to be sorrowful and sore troubled. Then saith he unto them, My soul is exceeding sorrowful, even unto death: abide ye here, and watch with me. And he went forward a little, and fell on his face, and prayed, saying, My Father, if it be possible, let this cup pass away from me: nevertheless, not as I will, but as thou wilt. And he cometh unto the disciples, and findeth them sleeping, and saith unto Peter, What, could ye not watch with me one hour? Watch and pray, that ye enter not into temptation: the spirit indeed is willing, but the flesh is weak. Again a second time he went away, and prayed, saying, My Father, if this cannot pass away, except I drink it, thy will be done. And he came again and found them sleeping, for their eyes were heavy. And he left them again, and went away, and prayed a third time, saying again the same words. Then cometh he to the disciples, and saith unto them, Sleep on now, and take your rest: behold, the hour is at hand, and the Son of man is betrayed into the hands of sinners. Arise, let us be going: behold, he is at hand that betrayeth me.—*Matt. 26: 36–46*

Loyalty always costs. It costs far more in the end to be loyal to the cause of evil; but it sometimes costs heavily to be loyal to the will of God. *In your life, are you willing to pay the price of loyalty to God?* If you are not, in the light of today's passage is there any real meaning in calling Jesus Master and Lord? Face frankly today the places where you have dodged the sacrifice that being true to God's will for you required you to make.

పోపోపో

Comment for the Week

To discuss theories about Jesus and to face Jesus himself are very different experiences, as different as is a debate over theories of ocean currents and trade winds from the real problem on the open sea. The one is intellectual, the other practical; the one involves ingenious thinking, the other prompt action. One feels the contrast when he moves back through all the theological discussions about Jesus until in the gospels he faces the Master himself. There he finds one who is impatient with those who hold even the highest opinion of him, unless they stand for the things which he represents. "Not every one that saith unto me, Lord, Lord," he cries, "but he that doeth the will of my Father" (Matt. 7: 21). He never welcomed ascriptions of praise unless they were accompanied by real loyalty to his Cause. Men called him "Good Master," "A teacher come from God," "Elijah," "One of the Prophets," and "John the Baptist risen from the dead"; his disciples called him "Messiah" and "Lord": but to all alike he insisted that not only imperfect but even adequate opinions of him were utterly unsatisfactory unless the men who held them were thoroughly devoted to the Cause for which he stood. Sir Robert Peel gave the poet-laureateship to Tennyson confessing, when he did so, that he had never read a line of Tennyson's poetry. His action was formal and official; it involved no deep personal appreciation of the one honored and no love of the beauty which he represented. How much praise of Jesus has been of this official character! Such applause meant no more to him than Pilate's reference to him as a "king." "Sayest thou this of thyself," Jesus asked Pilate, "or did others tell it thee concerning me?" (John 18: 34). The Master never would accept acclamation that was merely the borrowed result of other people's thinking. He insisted that men themselves should be utterly devoted to his Cause.

Now the explanation of this attitude of Jesus lies deep in his character. *He himself was absolutely loyal to a Cause.* Like the Mississippi through the center of the continent, gathering the contribution of the brooks and rivers upon every side, this central dedication of the Master flowed down through his life and everything was made to pay tribute to it. When Hannibal was nine years old, he swore before the altar of his gods eternal enmity to Rome, and that purpose mastered him until he died, and neither toil nor suffering nor failure could deflect him from it. In a loftier realm and in a nobler way Jesus had the same sort of resolute and undiscourageable devotion. At twelve he is already self-dedicated to his Father's business (Luke 2: 49); and throughout his ministry the abiding determination of his heart is manifest: "We must work the works of him that sent me, while it is day" (John 9: 4); "I must preach the good tidings of the kingdom of God to the other cities also" (Luke 4: 43); "My meat is to do the will of him that sent me" (John 4: 34). At last he "steadfastly set his face to go to Jerusalem," knowing well what would befall him there, and in Gethsemane pledged the last full payment of his loyalty. "Thy will, not mine, be done." We praise the *mind* and *heart* of the Master, his revelation of truth and his expression of love, but even more central to the understanding of him is the perception of the absolute devotion of his *will* to his Cause. This loyalty of his is like a recurring theme in the symphony of his life. There are wonderful passages of joy, terrible passages of tragedy, matchless recitatives of teaching, stirring harmonies of love, but ever reappearing through them all, underlying the entire composition of his life, was this master theme of loyalty.

Now the difficulty with accepting this idea of Jesus is that it takes a man nineteen centuries after Jesus, to suggest it first. Nobody who saw the Master seems to have suspected anything like this about him. The moneychangers, beaten by his stinging whip, the Pharisees, castigated by his scathing words, were not impressed by his "infinite sweetness, vague poetry, universal charm."

This conception of our Lord as himself utterly devoted to his Cause and calling others into the same consecration is essential to correcting certain misapprehensions of the Master's personality.

He has been called an ascetic, for example, a hater of familiar human happiness, calling men apart from home and ordinary relationships to save their souls. Did he not tell men to hate mother and father for his sake (Luke 14: 26); to pluck out eyes and cut off hands rather than risk the soul's welfare? (Matt. 5: 29, 30). Did he not command a rich young man to sell all that he had and give to the poor? (Matt. 19: 21). So Jesus was ascetic in tendency, men have said.

The answer to this is not simply to bring out another set of facts: that he was at home at a wedding-feast (John 2: 11); that he was caricatured by his enemies as "a gluttonous man and a winebibber" (Matt. 11: 19); that he did much of his greatest teaching at the dinner tables of his friends; that he loved flowers, loved children, loved the homelife of his followers. All we have said about his joy refutes the charge of asceticism. The real answer, however, is to see that when Jesus sets before his disciples a hard, self-denying life, demanding that even father, mother, children, houses or lands, should not stand between them and their allegiance to his Cause, he is not at all urging a monkish withdrawal from the world; he is rather a spiritual Garibaldi saying to his little band of patriots; "I promise you forced marches, short rations, bloody battles, wounds, imprisonment and death—let him who loves home and fatherland follow me." He is calling them to a dangerous campaign. He represents a Cause to which he is utterly loyal, and his note is that of a great leader, not an ascetic, when he says: Through exile from the synagogues, through trial before councils, through loss of property and family, through the baptism of blood that I shall be baptized with, follow me.

The leaders of a nation do not give themselves to anger, suborning witnesses and gathering mobs to cry, "Crucify him," to be rid merely of a "lovely character with a transporting countenance."

At the other extreme from those who call the Master an ascetic are those who insist that he was a poet. "His lovely character and doubtless one of those transporting countenances which sometimes appear in the Hebrew race, created round him a circle of fascination," says Renan. "Tenderness of heart was in him transformed into infinite sweetness, vague poetry, universal charm." Now the difficulty with accepting this idea of Jesus is that it takes a man nineteen centuries after Jesus, to suggest it first. Nobody who saw the Master seems to have suspected anything like this about him. The moneychangers, beaten by his stinging whip, the Pharisees, castigated by his scathing words, were not impressed by his "infinite sweetness, vague poetry, universal charm." When the Pharisees send soldiers to arrest him and those hardy and unimpressionable men join rather the circle of his listeners and go back to report failure because never man spake as he spake (John 7: 46); when his fellow villagers, angered at his preaching in the synagogues, take him out to slay him, and he walks unharmed through their midst, none daring to touch him (Luke 4: 14–30); when Hebrew fishermen, hearing him say, "Follow me," leave all to go after him, until at last even the sceptical Thomas says, "Let us also go, that we may die with him" (John 11: 16); when John the Baptist, stern, severe and strong, seeing him cries, "There cometh he that is mightier than I, the latchet of whose shoes I am not worthy to unloose"; how of all this shall "vague poetry" be the explanation?

The leaders of a nation do not give themselves to anger, suborning witnesses and gathering mobs to cry, "Crucify him," to be rid merely of a "lovely character with a transporting countenance." It has been the lot of poets to be neglected, starved, derided, but to be hated because they proposed to turn the world upside down, to be crucified with a superscription, "The King of the Jews," this is not for those who are content merely to see visions without executing them. The enemy of the Pharisees was no dreamer, but a soul of prodigious power, with twelve young men around him, to whom he was saying that the present age must pass away and a new order come, that Jerusalem would be destroyed and they be persecuted, but that the Kingdom would arrive, and that at all costs and hazards they must be loyal to the Cause. Jesus was not a Hegel, philosophizing unmoved within sound of the guns of Jena; he was a Leader planning the transformation of the world, and calling men to be patriots for his Kingdom. "I came to cast fire upon the earth," he said, "and what do I desire if it is already kindled?" (Luke 12: 49); "Think not that I came to send peace on the earth: I came not to send peace, but a sword" (Matt. 10: 34). The complaint of the chief priests against the Master was no charge to make against a dreamer: *"He stirreth up the people"* (Luke 23: 5).

I have inspired multitudes with such devotion that they would have died for me, but to do this it was necessary that I should be visibly present, with the electric influences of my looks, of my words, of my voice. Christ alone has succeeded in so raising the mind of man toward the unseen that it becomes insensible to the barriers of time and space.—Napoleon

---

This aspect of the Master's character would naturally impress a leader of men like Napoleon. Children delight in Jesus' care for children; home folk rejoice in his home-loving affection for Mary, Martha and Lazarus; friends study his friendships; but Napoleon thinks of him as a great leader, who had a Cause, and in the face of overwhelming handicaps made a success of it. How will a great general regard Jesus as a leader? "I have inspired multitudes with such devotion that they would have died for me," said Napoleon on St. Helena, "but to do this it was necessary that I should be visibly present, with the electric influences of my looks, of my words, of my voice. Christ alone has succeeded in so raising the mind of man toward the unseen that it becomes insensible to the barriers of time and space. Across a chasm of eighteen hundred years Jesus Christ makes a demand which is, above all others, difficult to satisfy. He asks for that which a philosopher may often seek in vain at the hands of his friends, or a father of his children, or a bride of her spouse, or a man of his brother. He asks for the human heart. He will have it entirely to Himself. He demands unconditionally, and forthwith His demand is granted. Wonderful! In defiance of time and space, the soul of man with all its powers becomes an annexation to the empire of Christ. All who sincerely believe in Him experience that remarkable super-natural love toward Him. This phenomenon is unaccountable; it is altogether beyond the scope of man's creative powers. Time, the great destroyer, is powerless to extinguish the sacred flame; time can neither exhaust its strength nor put a limit to its range. This it is which strikes me most. I have often thought of it. This it is which proves to me quite conclusively the divinity of Jesus Christ."

This aspect of our Lord's character, as a loyal devotee of a Cause gathering followers who share his loyalty, is reflected in his habitual thought of God. We continually emphasize the all-embracing knowledge and the boundless friendliness of God: "God is wisdom, God is love." But when we turn to Jesus we find another aspect of the divine nature made central—"The will of God." He speaks of God continually as one who has a purpose, a plan, a will for the whole world and for every life in it: "Whosoever shall do the will of God, the same is my brother, and sister, and mother" (Mark 3: 35); "My meat is to do the will of him that sent me, and to accomplish his work" (John 4: 34); "I seek not mine own will, but the will of him that sent me" (John 5: 30; 6: 38). When his disciples ask of him a prayer he puts in it his own great petition: "Thy kingdom come. Thy will be done, as in heaven, so on earth" (Matt. 6: 10). At last when his loyalty is evidently going to cost him the supreme sacrifice he says, "Not my will, but thine, be done." In his thought of God, wisdom and love are adjectives modifying God's will rather than nouns in their own right; the will of God is full of love: "It is not the will of your Father who is in heaven, that one of these little ones should perish" (Matt. 18: 14); and the will of God is wise: "Your Father knoweth what things ye have need of, before ye ask him." But primarily God was a God at work, "My Father worketh even until now, and I work" (John 5:17); he had a plan that gave meaning and purpose to all history, and Jesus' glory was that he knew that purpose and was absolutely loyal to his Father's plan. He believed that he and his followers were called on to build roadways over which the hosts of God would march in victory. He believed that he was the representative of the eternal purpose of God, the only thing in life worth living and dying for, and his enthusiastic loyalty is his dominant quality from the time he came into Galilee crying, "The kingdom of God is at hand," until he died for his Cause on Calvary. Missionaries tell us that in Japan, where loyalty is the supreme virtue, this quality of Jesus wins men to him most of all.

How distinct and unprecedented is this Christian thought of God you feel when you turn to ancient thought and ask concerning the future of the world. "What is the outcome going to be?" you ask the philosopher, and he has one answer: Cycles of existence, ever returning upon themselves, life moving in circles to work out old problems as it has worked them out before for the billionth time; no progress, no issue, no developing plot of the human drama that comes to its denouement; just endless circumferences around which life moves like a man lost in the woods who, vainly imagining himself to be coming out somewhere, finds himself at last back where he started. And when now facing the problem of human life you ask, "What then is a man's duty in such a world?" do you wonder that the noblest attitude toward life outside the Christian, namely, the Stoic morality, is even in its best representatives full of cries like this, "He who has seen the present has seen all that has been throughout eternity and all that will be throughout eternity"; "Whoever is forty years of age, if he but possess some understanding has in some sort seen all the past and all the future"; "The world is incessant change, life mere opinion and everything human is smoke"? In a word, in the pre-Christian thought of Greece and Rome you do not find any living hope about the future of the world. It is not going any whither; it is not coming out anywhere. The world is fixed in its recurring orbits by the fates. You cannot change it, you must fit yourself into it, and when you think of ultimate questions of meaning and destiny in human life you must content yourself with repeating after Prometheus, chained to the barren rock and fed upon by Jupiter's eagles:

… I must bear
What is ordained with patience, being aware
Necessity doth front the universe
With an invincible gesture.

All who sincerely believe in Him experience that remarkable super-natural love toward Him. This phenomenon is unaccountable; it is altogether beyond the scope of man's creative powers. Time, the great destroyer, is powerless to extinguish the sacred flame; time can neither exhaust its strength nor put a limit to its range. This it is which strikes me most. I have often thought of it. This it is which proves to me quite conclusively the divinity of Jesus Christ.—Napoleon

---

With Jesus, however, a new emphasis comes into human life. Wherever you find Christianity with any semblance of itself you hear this note. For it was a day rememberable forever in the annals of our race when Jesus came into Galilee preaching the good tidings of the Kingdom of God. *To him the world was coming out somewhere. This irrepressible conflict was not going to last forever. Two irreconcilable things could not remain permanently in the same universe, good and evil, God and Satan, life and death.* The world to him was a story that has a plot with progress in it and a climax. All the philosophic cycles become in his thought spirals, that seeming to return upon themselves move ever higher toward the summit. This is the inward soul of Jesus' preaching. God is purposing his Kingdom here. We are therefore like soldiers doing battle under a great general. We do not know all his plans but we trust him. We do not even understand all the supernal diplomacy that has made this war here necessary; that is the general's affair, not ours. *Our business is to fight under orders and help make every generation's battle another skirmish won in God's campaign.* We shall not do the ultimate winning; he must do that, and he will. He will wind up the age-long campaign some day with a strategic move that will startle heaven and earth together, and like Von Moltke at Sedan, catch the world's Napoleon in an unescapable trap. "Watch," says Jesus, "and again I say unto you, watch! the kingdom of God is at hand!"

This is the central passion of Jesus' life. If a man had tried to flatter Washington at Valley Forge, what would the great leader have said? Quick as a flash he would have turned to cry, *Where do you stand with reference to the cause which I represent?* So when men tried to flatter Jesus, he turned on them with a demand for loyalty to the Kingdom. A sentimental listener, superficially impressed, once cried, "Blessed is the womb that bare thee, and the breasts which thou didst suck!" and Jesus came back like lightning, "Yea rather, blessed are they that hear the word of God, and keep it" (Luke 11: 28). The Master was in the profoundest sense a Representative Man; he stood for a Cause and nothing would satisfy him but a man's allegiance to that same Purpose, loyalty to which was the glory of his life.

ঽঽঽ

Notes

5

The Master's Power of Endurance

One house may look as well as another on a fair day; but Jesus was a builder, and he knew that a storm reveals the kind of foundation underneath. When financial trouble comes, when plans fail, when death strikes the family, when accidents spoil cherished ambitions or health proves inadequate for the burdens assumed, how men's moral foundations are revealed!

Daily Readings

❖ **First Day, Fifth Week**

For what glory is it, if, when ye sin, and are buffeted for it, ye shall take it patiently? but if, when ye do well, and suffer for it, ye shall take it patiently, this is acceptable with God. For hereunto were ye called: because Christ also suffered for you, leaving you an example, that ye should follow his steps: who did no sin, neither was guile found in his mouth: who, when he was reviled, reviled not again; when he suffered, threatened not; but committed himself to him that judgeth righteously: who his own self bare our sins in his body upon the tree, that we, having died unto sins, might live unto righteousness; by whose stripes ye were healed.—*I Peter 2: 20–24*

Peter's recollection selects the uncomplaining fortitude of the Master for special emphasis. Jesus knew how to endure, and as Peter looks back, this seems to him one of the eminent marvels of his Lord's character. As we begin the study of Jesus' power of endurance, consider the need of patient courage in our own lives. For example, we all are handicapped, some by too little money, some by broken health or feeble constitutions, some by bereavement, some by unhappy heredity or cramping environment,—all of us by some unfortunate limitations, and sooner or later, as we saw last week, the man who lives up to his ideals has to pay the price of hostility against the customs of his day. *We are all called upon to live our lives in unideal situations that require patience, courage, persistent faith, and fortitude to deal with.* How well are you handling this aspect of your life's problem?

રે•રે•રે

❖ Second Day, Fifth Week

The men of Nineveh shall stand up in the judgment with this generation, and shall condemn it: for they repented at the preaching of Jonah; and behold, a greater than Jonah is here. The queen of the south shall rise up in the judgment with this generation, and shall condemn it: for she came from the ends of the earth to hear the wisdom of Solomon; and behold, a greater than Solomon is here.—*Matt. 12: 41, 42*

Therefore speak I to them in parables; because seeing they see not, and hearing they hear not, neither do they understand. And unto them is fulfilled the prophecy of Isaiah, which saith,

By hearing ye shall hear, and shall in no wise understand;
And seeing ye shall see, and shall in no wise perceive:
For this people's heart is waxed gross,
And their ears are dull of hearing,
And their eyes they have closed;
Lest haply they should perceive with their eyes,
And hear with their ears,
And understand with their heart,
And should turn again,
And I should heal them.—*Matt. 13: 13–15*

The Master faced a difficult situation in which to do his work. At times he might well have been discouraged. He had to deal with the universal human problem of making the best out of unideal conditions. Consider at once the temptation to resent bitterly the elements in our situation that we do not like, and to spend our time wishing that we were in some other estate. "They tell me," said a peculiarly lazy and weak man, "that I should be a good deal of a man if I lived in a different kind of a place." Can you imagine the Master considering such a futile attitude as even a possibility for his life? He made the best out of one of the most unideal situations that ever faced a great soul. He did not demand a different farm to labor on; he went to work on the farm that he had, and grew harvests on that, which have been feeding the world ever since. *His life sounds a courageous call to all of us: Stop whining; stop pitying yourself; see what you can do, by the help of God, with your unideal situation, for God never would have given it to you without some fine possibilities in it.*

રે•રે•રે

❖ Third Day, Fifth Week

And there come near unto him James and John, the sons of Zebedee, saying unto him, Teacher, we would that thou shouldst do for us whatsoever we shall ask of thee. And he said unto them, What would ye that I should do for you? And they said unto him, Grant unto us that we may sit, one on thy right hand, and one on thy left hand, in thy glory. But Jesus said unto them, Ye know not what ye ask. Are ye able to drink the cup that I drink? or to be baptized with the baptism that I am baptized with? And they said unto him, We are able. And Jesus said unto them, The cup that I drink ye shall drink; and with the baptism that I am baptized withal shall ye be baptized: but to sit on my right hand or on my left hand is not mine to give; but it is for them for whom it hath been prepared. And when the ten heard it, they began to be moved with indignation concerning James and John.—*Mark 10: 35–41*

If you had been the Master, how much patient endurance would you have shown toward disciples who so misunderstood you and who played selfish politics to get first place? *And yet Jesus used these very disciples to begin the Christianizing of the world!* What a parable of his problem and ours is that poem by Edward Sill:

This I beheld, or dreamed it in a dream:—
There spread a cloud of dust along a plain;
And underneath the cloud, or in it, raged
A furious battle, and men yelled, and swords
Shocked upon swords and shields. A prince's banner
Wavered, then staggered backward, hemmed by foes.
A craven hung along the battle's edge,
And thought, 'Had I a sword of keener steel—
That blue blade that the king's son bears—but this
Blunt thing!'—he snapt and flung it from his hand,
And lowering crept away and left the field.
Then came the king's son, wounded, sore bestead,
And weaponless, and saw the broken sword,
Hilt-buried in the dry and trodden sand,
And ran and snatched it, and with battle-shout
Lifted afresh he hewed his enemy down,
And saved a great cause that heroic day.

🪶🪶🪶

❖ Fourth Day, Fifth Week

And he came out, and went, as his custom was, unto the mount of Olives; and the disciples also followed him. And when he was at the place, he said unto them, Pray that ye enter not into temptation. And he was parted from them about a stone's cast; and he kneeled down and prayed, saying, Father, if thou be willing, remove this cup from me: nevertheless not my will, but thine, be done. And there appeared unto him an angel from heaven, strengthening him. And being in an agony he prayed more earnestly; and his sweat became as it were great drops of blood falling down upon the ground.—*Luke 22: 39–44*

There were times when the Master needed comfort, times when he had done his best and must face the inevitable. Do not such times come to all of us, when in the face of hostile circumstances we feel acutely the meaning of the fisher folk's saying, "Our skiffs are little and the sea is big"? Now the need of comfort is not an effeminate experience. Comfort comes from the same stem which is used in force, fort, fortify, fortitude. It is a strong and military word. The need of comfort is the need of inward fortification against the crushing circumstances of life. The Master was fortified; even from Gethsemane he came victorious. *Is it not true that sooner or later unavoidable trouble comes to everyone, and that it does one of two things,—either embitters him, leaving him resentful, discouraged, cynical; or else it ennobles him, leaving him humbler, kinder, with a deeper spiritual insight and a firmer trust in God?* Is not the difference inside the man himself?

ভাৰ ভাৰ ভাৰ

❖ Fifth Day, Fifth Week

And Jesus answereth them, saying, The hour is come, that the Son of man should be glorified. Verily, verily, I say unto you, Except a grain of wheat fall into the earth and die, it abideth by itself alone; but if it die, it beareth much fruit. He that loveth his life loseth it; and he that hateth his life in this world shall keep it unto life eternal. Now is my soul troubled; and what shall I say? Father, save me from this hour. But for this cause came I unto this hour. Father, glorify thy name.—*John 12: 23–25, 27, 28*

Every one therefore that heareth these words of mine, and doeth them shall be likened unto a wise man, who built his house upon the rock: and the rain descended, and the floods came, and the winds blew, and beat upon that house; and it fell not: for it was founded upon the rock. And every one that heareth these words of mine, and doeth them not, shall be likened unto a foolish man, who built his house upon the sand: and the rain descended, and the floods came, and the winds blew, and smote upon that house; and it fell: and great was the fall thereof.—*Matt. 7:24–27*

Sooner or later the storm of adverse circumstances falls on every man good or bad. What a testing of character adversity is! One house may look as well as another on a fair day; but Jesus was a builder, and he knew that a storm reveals the kind of foundation underneath. When financial trouble comes, when plans fail, when death strikes the family, when accidents spoil cherished ambitions or health proves inadequate for the burdens assumed, how men's moral foundations are revealed! *Have you underneath your life such an assurance that God cares most of all for spiritual success which is inward, and that he can help you to make even adversity contribute to character; have you such a conviction that, as Maltbie Babcock put it, "To be faithless is to fail, whatever the apparent success of earth; to be faithful is to succeed, whatever the apparent failure of earth;" are you, in a word, so deeply grounded in the faith of the Master, that you can stand unshaken in the day of storm?*

꙰꙰꙰

❖ Sixth Day, Fifth Week

And they bring him unto the place Golgotha, which is, being interpreted, The place of a skull. And they offered him wine mingled with myrrh: but he received it not. And they crucify him, and part his garments among them, casting lots upon them, what each should take. And it was the third hour, and they crucified him. And the superscription of his accusation was written over, THE KING OF THE JEWS. And with him they crucified two robbers; one on his right hand, and one on his left. And they that passed by railed on him, wagging their heads, and saying, Ha! thou that destroyest the temple, and buildest it in three days, save thyself, and come down from the cross. In like manner also the chief priests mocking him among themselves with the scribes said, He saved others; himself he cannot save. Let the Christ, the King of Israel, now come down from the cross, that we may see and believe. And they that were crucified with him reproached him.

And when the sixth hour was come, there was darkness over the whole land until the ninth hour. And at the ninth hour Jesus cried with a loud voice, *Eloi, Eloi, lama sabachthani?* which is, being interpreted, My God, my God, why hast thou forsaken me? And some of them that stood by, when they heard it, said, Behold, he calleth Elijah. And one ran, and filling a sponge full of vinegar, put it on a reed, and gave him to drink, saying, Let be; let us see whether Elijah cometh to take him down. And Jesus uttered a loud voice, and gave up the ghost.—*Mark 15: 22–37*

The cross of the Master, in which is symbolized all the sacrificial endurance of his life, has done more than all else put together to win the world to him. Nothing is so powerful as love that is willing to suffer to achieve its object. Recall Moses' words as he prays for his people: "Oh, this people have sinned a great sin! Yet now, if thou wilt forgive their sin—; and if not, blot me, I pray thee, out of thy book which thou hast written." *In this consuming devotion which identifies an individual with a cause, and makes him ready to give up everything selfish for the people whom he loves, lies the consummate perfection of character.* Consider the Master's life in the light of this truth, and then compare your own life with his sacrificial love.

☙☙☙

❖ Seventh Day, Fifth Week

But we have this treasure in earthen vessels, that the exceeding greatness of the power may be of God, and not from ourselves; we are pressed on every side, yet not straitened; perplexed, yet not unto despair; pursued, yet not forsaken; smitten down, yet not destroyed; always bearing about in the body the dying of Jesus, that the life also of Jesus may be manifested in our body.—*II Cor. 4: 7–10*

Wherefore we faint not; but though our outward man is decaying, yet our inward man is renewed day by day. For our light affliction, which is for the moment, worketh for us more and more exceedingly an eternal weight of glory; while we look not at the things which are seen, but at the things which are not seen: for the things which are seen are temporal; but the things which are not seen are eternal.—*II Cor. 4: 16–18*

Has not Paul in this passage caught perfectly the spirit of his Master? Jesus' courageous patience with undesirable situations and with the necessity of suffering sprang from his absolute trust in the good purpose of God. His task was to do the will of God for him; the consequences were God's responsibility and God would not fail to bring a worthy issue to all faithful work. Therefore the Master suffered patiently, endured courageously, sacrificed freely, labored hopefully, for he was sure that God was for him, and that no one ultimately could prevail against him. He looked even upon his death as a part of the plan of God, and resolutely said, Thy will, not mine. *Such trust as this is necessary to such character; you cannot have the result in hopeful fortitude without having the cause in faith; without reliance on God a man may be a cynic or a stoic, but he cannot be one who endures and sacrifices with glad confidence that "all things work together for good."*

☙☙☙

Comment for the Week

'Which is the more difficult task, the severer strain upon character, to win a victory, or to sustain a defeat and still keep undiscouraged and in good temper? There is no more searching test of the human spirit than the way it behaves when fortune is adverse and it has to pass through a prolonged period of disappointing failures. Then comes the real proof of the man. Achievement, if a man has the ability, is a joy; but to take hard knocks and come up smiting, to have your mainsail blown away and then to rig a sheet on the bowsprit and sail on, this is perhaps the deepest test of character.... *Life does not ask simply, How much can you do? It asks, also, How much can you endure, and still be unspoiled?*

No character is ultimately tested until it has suffered. It is a great deal easier to use our talents well than to use our troubles well, to achieve when we are prosperous than to be patient when we are in adversity.

We often speak of this quality as being "game." When a team, facing defeat, fights to the last second and never gives up; when a man plainly outraced sticks to his work and wins in the last lap by sheer grit,—these things rouse our special admiration, because we are ready to lionize any one who is "game." In human life this quality is absolutely essential to great character. When one reads the story of Prescott, the historian, accidentally blinded in a college frolic at Harvard, when he was fifteen years old, and still going on with his life work, refusing to be discouraged, we are stirred with admiration for his pluck. Pluck is an element in character that every one needs sooner or later, and without which no other elements are very impressive. Even when life starts prosperously, the time arrives at last when courage, hardihood, the power to endure unspoiled, are an absolute necessity; the day comes, as the Master said, when the rains descend, the floods come, and the winds blow. Sir Walter Scott's early life was exceedingly prosperous. He was an eminent poet, his novels were successful in an unprecedented way, his name was a word of mystery and charm over all of Europe, he built Abbotsford, grew wealthy and was knighted by the King. Then the storm came. First his publishers failed, involving him in a personal debt of 130,000 pounds; then his wife died; then his health broke. He described himself as "at sea in the dark and the vessel leaky, I think, into the bargain." To one who knows Sir Walter's bravery during those years of failure, his refusal to take advantage of a legal technicality to escape his debt, his patience, good cheer, unshaken faith in God, and undiscourageable work, the deep quality of his character is revealed then, more than in his days of achievement. *No character is ultimately tested until it has suffered. It is a great deal easier to use our talents well than to use our troubles well, to achieve when we are prosperous than to be patient when we are in adversity.*

If we are to understand the Master's character we must study it in this regard. Let us consider, therefore, the way his own saying, "The Son of man must suffer many things" (Mark 8: 31), came true in his life.

Think, for example, of the amazing hardihood and faith which Jesus showed in launching his great plan under utterly discouraging circumstances. Nothing is so hard for the leader of a cause to face as the necessity of dealing every day with circumstances that thwart and handicap him. When one stops to think of the conditions under which Jesus did his work, he is amazed. *There was the littleness of the field.* "From Dan to Beersheba" is with us a synonym for bigness, but from Dan to Beersheba was only 139 miles, and the whole of Palestine could be tucked into one half of New Hampshire. Mr. Hughes, author of *Tom Brown's School Days,* is not wrong when he says that if we take a province in India, where the native people are ruled by Maratha princes, as the Herods ruled Palestine, and where they in turn are superintended by a few English residents, as Pilate watched Jerusalem; and if we imagine some native out of such a province at the foothills of the Himalayas, emerging from his carpenter's shop to proclaim himself the Founder of an everlasting Kingdom, the legislator of a worldwide society, the Redeemer of humanity to God, we have a situation comparable to that which Jesus faced when he took up his work in Palestine. Under such outward conditions did the Master with amazing patience and faith begin his movement.

Then there was the inadequacy of the human instruments through which he had to work. Nothing so tries the patience of a sculptor as instruments that break in his hand or prove too coarse to express his meaning. The disciples have frankly left on record the fact that they were such instruments in the hands of Jesus. They were full of mean animosities that overflowed in desires for vengeance (Luke 9: 54); they so deeply believed in the Jewish laws about clean and unclean foods, that even Peter could not understand Jesus' insistence that it was spiritual quality, not ceremonial observance, that God wanted in his children (Mark 7: 14–19); they were so selfishly ambitious that they used to play politics in their desire for first place (Matt. 20: 20, 21; Mark 10: 35–37), and Luke tells us that this quarrel was continued even when they were sitting at the last supper (Luke 22: 24–26). Jesus had such a hard time to make them see his meaning that he said once to Peter, "Are ye also without understanding?" and on the last night he turned to Philip and said, "Have I been so long time with you, and dost thou not know me?" In the end one of them betrayed him, another denied him, and all the rest ran away. They have left this record of themselves.

Jesus picked out, after much prayer, the most faithful and efficient apostles that he could find, and these were the best (Luke 6: 12, 13). What a depth of unwearying patience the Master must have had to do his work through them!

Then there was the continual misunderstanding, slander and open hostility with which his work of saviorhood was met. To teach truth when one has the truth to teach, and to serve men when one is a friendly soul, are not only easy but are full of deepest satisfaction. Consider, however, what the Master must have endured when his truth was distorted and his friendliness slandered and abused. He was one who exalted spirit over body, with him the soul outbalanced all the world beside; and yet they called him a wine-bibber and a glutton. His life with God was the most reverent and intimate relationship that the imagination of man has ever tried to understand, and "Hallowed be thy name," is the natural expression of his adoration; but they called him a blasphemer (Matt. 9: 3). He was interested in no earthly kingdom for himself (Matt. 4: 8–10); he refused to take a crown or lead a revolt (John 6: 15); he was a Savior of the spiritual lives of men: but the Jews accused him of political ambitions, hired witnesses to swear to it, and raised a mob to cry "We have no king but Caesar." He was absolutely devoted to the truth, and even when death was the alternative, he held by his message; and yet they accused him of being a liar (John 7: 12). His was not a spirit of ill-will toward any man, however hostile, and yet they called him a servant of the devil (Matt. 12: 24), and even his own family mistrusted that he was losing his mind (Mark 3: 21). Consider the patient power of endurance that it requires to be thought crazy by your friends, to be excommunicated as a heretic by your church, to be condemned as a traitor by your country, and still to go on with undismayed faith and hope in God.

Then there was the certainty that his own earthly life was sure to end in a violent death, by crucifixion. At Caesarea Philippi he tells his disciples plainly what he foresees must happen to him, that he will be crucified (Mark 8: 31). It is well to consider that Jesus had probably seen men crucified. Let a man stand before some great picture of the crucifixion like that of Rubens in Antwerp; let him imagine that he had himself seen such a thing done to a human being and knew that it was going to be done to him; and he can a little understand the conditions under which the latter part of Jesus' ministry was passed. As Rubens pictures it, one thief is gasping for breath; the other, struck upon the leg by a Roman soldier to see if he is dead, is crying out in a sudden access of agony, and writhing, tears one foot loose from the nail that pierced it; the Master's mother and John are weeping with averted eyes, unable to endure the sight, and Mary Magdalene, in passionate grief, is trying with vain hands to ward away the soldier who from horseback drives the spear into the Savior's side; the body of the Master hangs limp and dead. *Jesus had probably seen crucifixions, and knew that he was going to be crucified.* Our words fortitude, courage, and patient resolution need an expanded meaning before they are qualified to cover the case.

Think of the times when the Master, trying to get with his disciples to understand him and failing, forced to say even at the end, "I have many things to tell you, but ye cannot bear them now."

Doubtless, even a greater burden on the Master's heart than his own suffering was the fact that he and his Cause were sure to involve his followers in suffering. The Master would find it easier to endure hardship himself than to be the occasion of it to others. When, at Gethsemane's gate, he turns to the officers and says, "I am he; if therefore ye seek me, let these go their way" (John 18: 8), he is speaking out of his love's instinctive wish, even in the midst of his own grief, to spare his friends. We often emphasize how much the Master's friendship meant to those who belonged to his inner circle; but it is worth considering that their friendship meant not a little to him. He called them his friends (John 15: 13–15) he counted on their companionship in the profoundest experiences of his life (Matt. 26: 36, 37); he loved them so really that when he was alone he was often praying for them (Luke 22: 32); he was grateful for even their inadequate help and said at the end in thanks, "Ye are they that have continued with me in my temptations" (Luke 22: 28). When the final crisis came he craved their fellowship: "With desire I have desired to eat this Passover with you before I suffer" (Luke 22: 15). And when he thought of the progress of his work after his death, he relied with wonderful confidence upon his friends. The Master has been called the "Specialist in Friendship," and he was, with an affectionate loyalty, whose depths our imaginations with difficulty plumb. If one of us loved his friends as the Master did, so that he could sum up the commandment of love, "That ye love one another, even as I have loved you," what do you suppose it would mean to us to involve those friends in calumny and persecution? This was one of the burdens on the heart of Jesus. He often spoke of it. "They will deliver you up to councils, and in their synagogues they will scourge you;... and ye shall be hated of all men for my name's sake" (Matt. 10: 17, 22; Mark 13 9ff); "Men shall hate you, and... shall separate you from their company, and reproach you, and cast out your name as evil, for the Son of man's sake" (Luke 6: 22); "They shall put you out of the synagogues: yea, the hour cometh, that whosoever killeth you shall think that he offereth service unto God" (John 16: 2); "The cup that I drink ye shall drink; and with the baptism that I am baptized withal shall ye be baptized" (Mark 10: 39). Jesus had no illusions about the sacrifice which his movement was going to cost his friends. Can you measure the burden that this meant to the spirit of the Master?

In addition to these many ways in which the Son of Man had to suffer, *there was the necessary loneliness of his own life.* "To be great is to be misunderstood," says Emerson. The altitude of a mountain is the measure of its solitude, for as it eminence increases it overpasses the companionship of lesser peaks. This is true even of worldly position, and Tennyson said, after one of his last interviews with Queen Victoria, "She is so lonely on that height; it is terrible!" Consider then the altitude and solitude of the Master's spirit. The situation in Gethsemane is typical of his whole life; the world, outside, alien and hostile; a few of his disciples at the garden gate, sympathetic but dull of understanding; Peter, James and John closer to the Master and comprehending more his purpose and his struggle; but far beyond them all, under the trees, Jesus himself, fighting out his battle alone with God! Think of the times when the Master, trying to get with his disciples to understand him and failing, forced to say even at the end, "I have many things to tell you, but ye cannot bear them now," must have longed for the sympathetic companionship of some human friend who really could enter into his profoundest purposes and share his spiritual experiences.

Review in your thought now the burdens of the Master: the discouraging handicaps of the Jewish field in which he worked, the inadequacy of the men who were his instruments, the calumny and hostility with which his saviorhood was greeted, the imminent certainty of his own crucifixion and the persecution of his friends, and finally the loneliness of his own soul. From what you know of men, what would be the natural effect of such a cumulation of burdens and hostilities? Would you not expect any one so circumstanced to be *gloomy and morose?* Yet, consider that all we said of the Master's joy is true, in the face of all this array of troubles. His radiant cheer was never submerged by them. Would you not expect any one under such conditions to grow *anxious, worrying over his threatened work?* Yet the Master's confidence never wavered. Even when Mary Magdalene anointed his feet with ointment, and he said that it was for his burial, he added, *"Wheresoever this gospel shall be preached in the whole world,* that also which this woman hath done shall be spoken of for a memorial of her"* (Matt. 26: 12, 13). Can you easily imagine anyone facing what the Master faced without *becoming cynical and discouraged?* Doctor Jefferson has noted in this connection the words of Lord Randolph Churchill in a letter to his wife in 1891: "More than two-thirds, in all probability, of my life is over, and I will not spend the remainder of my years in beating my head against a stone wall. There has been no consideration, no indulgence, no memory or gratitude—nothing but spite, malice and abuse. I am quite tired and dead sick of it all, and will not continue political life any longer." In the light of this natural human outburst, think of the patience, the persistent faith, the unconquerable good will of the Master. Would you not expect any one, enduring what he endured in a good cause, to have *his faith in God shaken?* Trouble strips a man of all his borrowed faith and drives him in on his own resources. In prosperity a man may believe in God in common with his friends and may rejoice in social worship; but in trouble, all artificial props are knocked away, and he can rely on no more faith than that which he possesses in himself. Joy says *we;* sorrow says *I.* Joy says, "Come worship the Lord with me and let us exalt his name together." Sorrow says, "O *my* God, *my* soul is cast down within *me.*" Think of how many people find that they have no real faith when they are so driven in upon themselves. Then consider the Master's perfect reliance on his Father, even in the agonies of crucifixion saying, "Into thy hands I commend my spirit."

What think ye of Christ? Is it any wonder that the Church's thought has been irresistibly drawn to him as the fulfilment of Isaiah's fifty-third chapter?

ತಿ ತಿ ತಿ

Notes

6

The Master's Sincerity

The Rabbis had prejudices; he could have trimmed his utterances so as not to have aroused them. The Sadducees and the Pharisees had characteristic sins; he could have spoken to them about something else. And he could have excused this attitude on the ground that it was better for the sake of his work. On the contrary, the Master's steadfast habit was to tell the plain truth, no matter who was alienated.

Daily Readings

❖ **First Day, Sixth Week**

And the Lord said, Forasmuch as this people draw nigh unto me, and with their mouth and with their lips do honor me, but have removed their heart far from me, and their fear of me is a commandment of men which hath been taught them; therefore, behold, I will proceed to do a marvellous work among this people, even a marvellous work and a wonder; and the wisdom of their wise men shall perish, and the understanding of their prudent men shall be hid.

Woe unto them that hide deep their counsel from Jehovah, and whose works are in the dark, and that say, Who seeth us? and who knoweth us?—*Isaiah 29: 13–15*

Ye hypocrites, well did Isaiah prophesy of you, saying,

This people honoreth me with their lips;

But their heart is far from me.

But in vain do they worship me,

Teaching as their doctrines the precepts of men.—*Matt. 15: 7–9*

Note that one of the strongest passages in the prophets against hypocrisy is a favorite with the Master. We can picture him reading and pondering it, and, not content with its historical reference, seeking the meaning of the same spirit in his own day. Let us this week catch for ourselves the Master's feeling about sincerity and hypocrisy, and let us think of the new forms in which they clothe themselves in our generation. It is easy to condemn the Pharisees now; they are dead. *But it will cost a searching struggle for some of us to give up our own contentment with the approval of man, who "looketh on the outward appearance," and seek inwardly to be such persons that we have the approval of God, who "looketh on the heart."*

❧❧❧

❖ Second Day, Sixth Week

But all their works they do to be seen of men: for they make broad their phylacteries, and enlarge the borders of their garments, and love the chief place at feasts, and the chief seats in the synagogues, and the salutations in the marketplaces, and to be called of men, Rabbi. But be not ye called Rabbi: for one is your teacher, and all ye are brethren. And call no man your father on the earth: for one is your Father, even he who is in heaven. Neither be ye called masters: for one is your master, even the Christ.— *Matt. 23: 5–10*

In the light of this passage define the hypocrisy that Jesus so much abhorred. *Does it not consist in caring little for the real goodness and usefulness of life, so long as an admirable, or at least respectable, appearance can be maintained?* How modern this sin is! Some one has written: "He stands having his loins girt about with religiosity and having on the breastplate of respectability. His feet are shod with ostentatious philanthropy, his head is encased in the helmet of spread-eagle patriotism. Holding in his left hand the buckler of worldly success and in his right the sword of 'influence,' he is able to withstand in the evil day, and having done all, to stand." Compare this picture with the original portrait in Ephesians 6: 10ff, for which the Master himself might have sat.

❧❧❧

❖ Third Day, Sixth Week

When therefore thou doest alms, sound not a trumpet before thee, as the hypocrites do in the synagogues and in the streets, that they may have glory of men. Verily I say unto you, They have received their reward. But when thou doest alms, let not thy left hand know what thy right hand doeth:... and thy Father who seeth in secret shall recompense thee.

And when ye pray, ye shall not be as the hypocrites: for they love to stand and pray in the synagogues and in the corners of the streets, that they may be seen of men. Verily I say unto you, They have received their reward. But thou, when thou prayest, enter into thine inner chamber, and having shut thy door, pray to thy Father who is in secret, and thy Father who seeth in secret shall recompense thee.—*Matt. 6: 2–6*

The secret of hypocrisy is the desire to *appear well* without paying the price that *being right* costs. We love to be highly regarded by men; we make their approval our standard; and we learn that we can meet this standard, for a while at least, by outward appearance. *It is of this that Jesus is thinking in Luke 16: 15, "Ye are they that justify yourselves in the sight of men; but God knoweth your hearts."* Think frankly of ways you have deliberately tried to cover the real truth by outward appearance, for the sake of gaining approval in your family, in your college classroom, in your church. Consider the ignobility of this; and, in contrast, the nobility of being a person of whom those who know him best may say, as Spurgeon said of Gladstone: "We believe in no man's infallibility, but it is restful to feel sure of one man's integrity."

❧❧❧

❖ Fourth Day, Sixth Week

Ye are the salt of the earth: but if the salt have lost its savor, wherewith shall it be salted? it is thenceforth good for nothing, but to be cast out and trodden under foot of men. Ye are the light of the world. A city set on a hill cannot be hid. Neither do men light a lamp, and put it under the bushel, but on the stand; and it shineth unto all that are in the house. Even so let your light shine before men; that they may see your good works, and glorify your Father who is in heaven.—*Matt. 5: 13–16*

Take heed that ye do not your righteousness before men, to be seen of them: else ye have no reward with your Father who is in heaven.

When therefore thou doest alms, sound not a trumpet before thee, as the hypocrites do in the synagogues and in the streets, that they may have glory of men.—*Matt. 6: 1, 2*

How do you explain this apparent self-contradiction of Jesus? He tells us so to live that *men may see* our good works; and then he warns us not to do our righteousness *to be seen* of men. Does not the explanation lie in the fact that there are two kinds of hypocrisy? With the latter sort, where a man tries to appear *better* than he is, we are familiar; but we must face the former kind, where a man is willing to appear *worse* than he is. If a man is a follower of Christ in secret, but will not confess him and publicly stand for him; if he lets himself be regarded by some as possibly not in earnest about his faith and character when in fact he is in earnest, is not he a hypocrite? *It is hypocrisy to appear worse than you ore. It is a man's duty to market his, best goods, to reveal his best self, to let the finest things that God has wrought in him, shine forth.*

ลงลงลง

❖ Fifth Day, Sixth Week

Again, ye have heard that it was said to them of old time, Thou shalt not forswear thyself, but shalt perform unto the Lord thine oaths: but I say unto you, Swear not at all; neither by the heaven, for it is the throne of God; nor by the earth, for it is the footstool of his feet; nor by Jerusalem, for it is the city o the great King. Neither shalt thou swear by thy head, for thou canst not make one hair white or black. But let your speech be, Yea, yea; Nay, nay: and whatsoever is more than these is of the evil one.— *Matt. 5: 33–37*

Consider the reasons for the Master's praise of unaffected genuineness in speech. Think of our dependence upon words for our understanding of one another, and think of the shattering of confidence and the growth of cynical suspicion which follow the discovery that we have been deceived. Many a man becomes a hard rock covered with the soft moss of words, and we never learn how hard the rock is until we slip on the moss and fall down. Such men break up the mutual relationship of trust on which all worthy human life depends; they are the arch traitors against the race. *Have you grown lax about insincere and deceptive speech? Or do you hate a lie as the Master did, so that your friends know that they can depend absolutely upon what you say?*

ลงลงลง

❖ Sixth Day, Sixth Week

Moreover when ye fast, be not, as the hypocrites, of a sad countenance: for they disfigure their faces, that they may be seen of men to fast. Verily I say unto you, They have received their reward. But thou, when thou fastest, anoint thy head, and wash thy face; that thou be not seen of men to fast, but of thy Father who is in secret: and thy Father, who seeth in secret, shall recompense thee.—*Matt. 6: 16–18*

Does not this passage reveal, as verse six of this same chapter does, the secret of the Master's inner life? He lived in fellowship with the *"Father who seeth in secret."* He brought all questions to that inner court for settlement; he was satisfied with no deed that did not merit the approval of the Father, who "looketh on the heart"; *he was content only with being right in the sight of God.* Consider the value of secret prayer as a means of detecting shams in our own lives, of making us discontented with ourselves until we are inwardly in harmony with the will of God for us, and so of making us genuinely sound and good. Moral cosmetics cannot avail us in the presence of God; "Be not deceived, God is not mocked." Therefore for the sake of our characters' genuineness, let us put ourselves continually to the test of quiet meditation and prayer.

෨෨෨

❖ Seventh Day, Sixth Week

Beware of false prophets, who come to you in sheep's clothing, but inwardly are ravening wolves. By their fruits ye shall know them. Do men gather grapes of thorns, or figs of thistles? Even so every good tree bringeth forth good fruit; but the corrupt tree bringeth forth evil fruit. A good tree cannot bring forth evil fruit, neither can a corrupt tree bring forth good fruit. Every tree that bringeth not forth good fruit is hewn down, and cast into the fire. Therefore by their fruits ye shall know them. Not everyone that saith unto me, Lord, Lord, shall enter into the kingdom of heaven; but he that doeth the will of my Father who is in heaven.
—Matt. 7: 15–21

After you have read this searching passage, how naturally the prayer comes, "Create in me a clean heart, O God; and renew a right spirit within me." A man can do an unselfish deed occasionally by force of will; but can a man really be *unselfish,* without being continually "transformed by the renewing of his mind"? *Jesus says that good deeds or words which do not spring out of the nature and quality of the heart are not genuinely good.* So Paul cries: "If I give all my goods to feed the poor, but *have not love,* it profiteth me nothing." When a man accepts this ideal of a life inwardly and genuinely right in its attitude and quality, he is at once thrown back on God. As well might a tree try to be sound without drawing on the physical energies that are around it, as a man might expect to be inwardly good without appropriating the help of the Spirit of God.

෨෨෨

Comment for the Week

What the Master endured for his Cause we have seen in the last chapter, and that endurance is in itself a sufficient testimony to the utter sincerity of our Lord's devotion. Hardship severely tests the genuineness of loyalty, especially when a cause has little human probability of winning; and the Master was steadfast when nothing but absolute devotion to duty could have been his motive. But sincerity in Jesus involved something more than consecration; it was the pervasive quality of his whole life. Some virtues are like separate flowers, they beautify the spiritual landscape; a few are like the climate, they are the atmosphere in which all the other virtues grow. Sincerity was the climate of the Master's spirit.

Nothing else can ever be right in a man's life, if he is not sincere. A lie is the fundamental sin. No man ever can really *see* another; we are all invisible personalities, inhabiting our bodies; and we signal to one another by words, looks, actions. A man who lies deliberately hangs out a wrong signal. He creates distrust as to the dependableness of any other signals he may ever make, and he disarranges the whole system of mutual confidence upon which human life depends. When the lie has worked back into the quality of his life, until he *is* a deceptive man, he has made impossible in himself any fine virtue whatsoever. How Jesus felt about this matter is clear from his definition of the devil: "When he speaketh a lie, he speaketh of his own: for he is a liar, and the father thereof" (John 8: 44).

The secret of hypocrisy is the desire to *appear well* without paying the price that *being right* costs.

To understand the depth of the Master's passion for truth and hatred of insincerity, we must watch his actions under circumstances where ordinary men are sorely tempted to lie.

Think of him in Pilate's court, with the Roman procurator rather kindly disposed to him, and the mob outside crying for his crucifixion. Put yourself in his place, and consider the excuses that would have suggested themselves to justify a lie. See how easily compromise statements could have been constructed that would have offered some hope of mollifying Pilate and effecting release. How clearly, then, is the attitude of the Master toward a lie revealed in his affirmation that he is the Christ, and in his further fearless assertion: "To this end have I been born, and to this end am I come into the world, that I should bear witness unto the truth" (John 18: 37). *He would not lie even to save himself from the cross.* Moreover his scorn of insincerity, even when critical circumstances seem to offer an excuse, is revealed in the reproachful look that he gave Peter after that disciple had denied him (Luke 22: 55–62). Conditions that would be a severer strain upon any one's devotion to truth can hardly be imagined than the trial and crucifixion of the Master. Is it too much to say that in view of his attitude then, *there are no imaginable circumstances under which Jesus would have deceived any one?*

We can trace this same attitude back into all his dealing with the leaders of the Jews. When one considers the Master's passionate desire to have his revelation of the Father welcomed, his principles of life accepted in the private and social life of men, he feels at once the implied temptation by all means to avoid arousing the hostility of influential people. If he could have won over the Rabbis, if he even could have persuaded them to neutrality, think how much easier his work would have been, how much more rapidly his Gospel would have spread among the people! The Rabbis had prejudices; he could have trimmed his utterances so as not to have aroused them. The Sadducees and the Pharisees had characteristic sins; he could have spoken to them about something else. And he could have excused this attitude on the ground that it was better for the sake of his work. On the contrary, the Master's steadfast habit was to tell the plain truth, no matter who was alienated. He spoke to men who overemphasized religious form and minimized spiritual reality, and he insisted that their religion was sham (Luke 11: 42); he attacked strongly intrenched ideas of Sabbath observance although the Pharisees and Herodians became so angry that they sought to kill him (Mark 3: 1–6); he preached to the rich in such pointed and scathing words that "the Pharisees, who were lovers of money,... scoffed at him" (Luke 16: 14); and in the presence of impenitent duplicity his denunciation was untamed by prudence. *Any one who follows the Master through his fearless ministry will be unable to escape the impression of absolute genuineness. Here was one who could neither be bought nor frightened, one who, even, that good might come, would not tell a lie.*

Consider the passages quoted in the last chapter, where Jesus forewarned even his diminished band of followers of the persecutions that lay ahead of them, and see how clear the impression is that here is one, who, when the success of his life-work seems to be at stake and his supporters are deserting him, will not even by silence deceive any one. In the light of this attitude of Jesus, measure, if you can, his hatred of a lie.

An even deeper evidence of the Master's inner and perfect sincerity is given us in his attitude toward men who wanted to be his disciples. How much he desired followers, how radiant he was with satisfaction when anyone was willing to become a loyal servant of his Cause, is shown continually, as when Zacchaeus repented (Luke 19: 2ff), or when the Greeks through Philip sought a conference (John 12: 20–23). How sorry he was to lose a possible disciple is seen in his regret when the rich ruler refused the necessary sacrifice that discipleship required (Luke 18: 22–24). *He needed followers, and all too few were willing to support him and his work.* Nevertheless, when a scribe said to him, "Teacher, I will follow thee whithersoever thou goest," he answered at once, "The foxes have holes, and the birds of the heaven have nests; but the Son of man hath not where to lay his head" (Matt. 8: 19, 20). He would take no disciple under false pretences; he presented plainly the difficulties and hazards of the work. In the height of his popularity there "went with him great multitudes." Consider then his spirit when he turned and said to them: "If any man cometh unto me, and hateth not his own father, and mother, and wife, and children, and brethren, and sisters, yea, and his own life also, he cannot be my disciple. Whosoever doth not bear his own cross, and come after me, cannot be my disciple" (Luke 14: 26, 27). Consider the utter sincerity of these words. This was one of the greatest sacrifices that the Master ever made, for, as John tells us, the multitudes disappeared, fearing the cost of following him, until at last to the twelve who alone remained, Jesus said, "Would ye also go away?" (John 6: 66, 67). *At all costs, he told the truth, even about the dangers that awaited his disciples.* Consider the passages quoted in the last chapter, where Jesus forewarned even his diminished band of followers of the persecutions that lay ahead of them, and see how clear the impression is that here is one, who, when the success of his life-work seems to be at stake and his supporters are deserting him, will not even by silence deceive any one. In the light of this attitude of Jesus, measure, if you can, his hatred of a lie.

The most subtle kind of insincerity, however, does not consist in deliberate willingness to mislead others; it consists rather in complacently allowing outward forms to be substituted for a genuine, inward life. It is one thing never to *speak* insincerely; it is a deeper thing always to insist on *being sincere.* This deeper meaning is Jesus' thought when he says, "Ye shall not be as the hypocrites" (Matt. 6: 5). Over against the sort of life that substituted assumed appearance for inner reality, Jesus insisted on unaffected genuineness. The Sermon on the Mount should be read in this connection, not first as a new code of precepts for us, but as a revelation of the sort of inner life which the Master himself really lived. We learn, then, that to refrain from outward acts of hostility toward our brethren may be only theatrical, but that Jesus required of himself a genuine, positive love of others (Matt. 5: 21–26). We learn that from outward acts of impurity a man may refrain as a sheer *tour de force* of will, in obedience to law, but that Jesus was content only with a life of unsmirched thought, of inward purity (Matt. 5: 27, 28). We learn that truthfulness may be externalized until it is a mere matter of keeping formal oaths, but that Jesus was satisfied only with a life of transparent candor, whose simplest expressions could be depended on utterly (Matt. 5: 33–37). We learn that philanthropic giving may be merely an ostentatious display, and that it awakened the Master's scorn, unless it proceeded, as in him, from a sincere care for men, delighting most in service rendered privately (Matt. 6: 1–4). Even prayer, the Master says, may be theatrical, offered for the applause of men, but his own prayer-life is an invisible fellowship with God, that finds its hours of richest communion in quiet places where men cannot see (Matt. 6: 5, 6). We learn that religious observances, like fasting, may become so formal that they have no more spiritual value than acting a part in a play, but that with him, the religious life was a deep and inward experience, and a genuine communion of soul with God (Matt. 6: 16–18). The Sermon on the Mount is rightly regarded as the Master's most characteristic utterance, and it is the revelation of a life whose central passion was genuineness. What he teaches here in words, he taught by symbol when he placed before his disciples, as their ideal, the simple, unaffected sincerity of a child (Mark 9: 36).

When we endeavor to analyze such love of reality in word and life as Jesus exhibited, we find two elements in it, the first of which we may call self-respect. *We all delight in being respected by others, but the Master's character suggests a more searching rule, to be such persons in our inward life that we can respect ourselves.* A paste diamond, large and brilliant, may gain the admiration of the unwary spectator, but it cannot respect itself. A man who has "bluffed" a recitation or has "cribbed" an examination, may win a high mark, but he cannot respect himself. A professional athlete who has passed himself off as an amateur may be carried on the shoulders of a college crowd in triumph, but he knows inwardly that he is shamming and he does not respect himself. So to live that a deep self-respect is possible means a thoroughly genuine life.

Let any man test himself by this standard and he will see in how many places in his life, his

… highest conscience is, not to leave't undone,
But to keep't unknown."

He endeavors to live in such a way as to escape the condemnation of his fellows, or, if he is more positive in character, in such a way as to win their approval. Such a motive is clearly a great help to the moral life, but it inevitably tends to insincerity unless the deeper motive lies behind it: to live such a life that we are not ashamed of what we think and are and do in the dark. Ruskin tells us that in one corner of a Venetian church he found the statue of a doge.[1] The side toward the audience was elaborately finished; the side toward the corner was left rough. On the public side, the forehead was carefully wrinkled, the cap beautifully chased, the ermine robe scrupulously imitated; on the dark side the marble was unwrought. "Now," says Ruskin, "comes the very gist and point of the whole matter. This lying monument is at least veracious, if in nothing else, in its testimony to the character of the sculptor. He was banished from Venice for forgery in 1487." Study the moral decline of this sculptor as here disclosed, and see that his outward disgrace began with the failure of self-respect and so of genuineness.

1. Editor: In the republics of Genoa and Venice, a "doge" was the chief magistrate.

With this thought in mind, turn to the Master's character. He is showing the quality of his own spirit when he scorns those who do their "righteousness before men to be seen of them" (Matt. 6: 1); when he says to the Pharisees, "Ye are they that justify yourselves in the sight of men; but God knoweth your hearts" (Luke 16: 15); when he insists that the real evil in human life lies back in the secret thoughts and not in faulty ceremonial (Matt. 15: 19, 20), and that a man's inner life must be cleansed before he is genuinely good (Matt. 12: 34, 35). The Master was sincere in this sense, that he welcomed such thoughts, cherished such ambitions, held such inward feelings about his fellows that *he never had to be ashamed of himself.* The seers of the race all join with Sidney Lanier in noting this crystalline purity and genuineness of Jesus:

What least defect or shadow of defect,

What rumor, tattled by an enemy

Of inference loose, what lack of grace

Even in torture's grasp, or sleep's or death's—

what amiss may I forgive in Thee,

Jesus, good Paragon, thou Crystal Christ?

The other element in the genuineness of the Master is revealed in his phrase, *"The Father who seeth in secret."* We are chiefly aware of the public opinion of men: he lived in the consciousness of the Public Opinion of the Universe, and he cared first of all for the latter. In the fine phrase of Scripture he lived "in the sight of God." Now, when a man brings all his thoughts, ambitions, motives, and heart attitudes to the arbitrament of the "Father who seeth in secret," he must be a genuine man. Many of us are like a rock in the woods, covered with trailing vines and externally attractive, but turn us over and what a scampering of unclean, crawling things to their holes! This is Tennyson's meaning when he says,

Do we indeed desire the dead

Should still be near us at our side?

Is there no baseness we would hide?

No inner vileness that we dread?

But that God knows our hearts is not a vague possibility, like the immediate presence of the dead; it is a certain fact. That we live on good terms with our fellows may not be a test of sincerity at all; that we live on honorable terms with ourselves, is a far deeper standard; that we live on right terms with God, means absolute genuineness of life. Are we even endeavoring to standardize our spirits by that test?

On the contrary, consider the ways in which we keep just within the boundaries of social respectability, and are content with that. Think how a man may sit in his quiet room, where no law would think of touching him, where there is no sound of outward revelry, and there may conjure with his thoughts or with an evil book until within his sober body his drunken soul reels on from vice to vice, and he knows in imagination what the roués[2] of the world have felt in their most dissipated hours. Think how men in college games and in business come just as near to foul play as they dare. How often do we crowd up close to the fence of respectability's limit, and push our faces between the pickets, wishing that we had courage to climb to the other side! Many a man's goodness consists in being as bad as he dares, and all of us must confess that the test of self-respect and of "The Father who seeth in secret," spoils our self-complacency and fills us with shame.

This is the innermost marvel of our Master's life, appreciated all the more when we contrast it with our own, that his life with God was never to him a cause of shame. "This is my beloved Son, in whom I am well pleased," was God's attitude toward him: "I do always the things that are pleasing to him" (John 8: 29) was his consciousness of true filial life with God. In a word, the glory of the Master is the absolute genuineness of his life.

The sincerity of Jesus, therefore, has at least these elements in it: he would under no circumstances deceive anyone whether to save himself, to allay hostility against his Cause, or to win followers; and he was content only with an inward life, so genuinely good, that he needed never to be ashamed of himself nor to shrink from the eye of his Father. What sort of character do you estimate that it requires not only to hold such an ideal but to convince the world that that ideal has been actually achieved?

The bearing which this absolute sincerity of the Master has upon our confidence in him is clear. When our Lord tells us that he has a unique relationship with God, that he really knows the truth about him and can tell it to us, one essential ground of our trust in the revelation is the genuineness of the Revealer. That the Master out of a real experience was interpreting to us the truth about God, has behind it all the confirming power of his utter candor and sincerity. *"If I should say I know him not,"* John reports him to have said to the Pharisees, *"I shall be like unto you, a liar"* (John 8: 55).

࿊࿊࿊

2. Editor: a roué is a man who has given over his life to sensual pleasure.

7

The Master's Self-Restraint

To be gifted with supernal powers and never to use them self-ishly; to be sent on a divine mission and never to expect God to stop the lions' mouths; to be offered a temporal kingdom and to be crucified for a spiritual one, that was the temptation and triumph of Jesus.

Daily Readings

❖ First Day, Seventh Week

Wherefore it behooved him in all things to be made like unto his brethren, that he might become a merciful and faithful high priest in things pertaining to God, to make propitiation for the sins of the people. For in that he himself hath suffered being tempted, he is able to succor them that are tempted.—*Hebrews 2: 17, 18*

For we have not a high priest that cannot be touched with the feeling of our infirmities; but one that hath been in all points tempted like as we are, yet without sin. Let us therefore draw near with boldness unto the throne of grace, that we may receive mercy, and may find grace to help us in time of need.—*Hebrews 4: 15, 16*

Consider the truth in these passages, that if the Master's character is to have vital significance for us, if we are to be encouraged to take it for our Ideal and are to depend on the Spirit, whose work it was, to achieve a like quality in us, the character must be the result of moral struggle. *We can neither understand nor imitate a character that is not tempted. An untempted Christ would be outside our moral world altogether.* Let us try this week to appreciate the fact that Jesus was tremendously tempted "in all points like as we are." You cannot imagine joy as a virtue except in the presence of the temptation to be discouraged; nor magnanimity as a virtue except where a soul is tempted to be vengeful; nor loyalty except where one is tempted to desert his Cause. Remember then as you face your moral struggles that whatever the Master's character was, it was that only by dint of a great battle against the opposite.

No, when the fight begins within himself,
A man's worth something. God stoops o'er his head,
Satan looks up between his feet—both tug—
He's left, himself, i' the middle: the soul wakes
And grows.

೫ ೫ ೫

❖ Second Day, Seventh Week

And Jesus, full of the Holy Spirit, returned from the Jordan, and was led in the Spirit in the wilderness during forty days being tempted of the devil. And he did eat nothing in those days: and when they were completed, he hungered. And the devil said unto him, If thou art the Son of God, command this stone that it become bread. And Jesus answered unto him, It is written, Man shall not live by bread alone. And he led him up, and showed him all the kingdoms of the world in a moment of time. And the devil said unto him, To thee will I give all this authority, and the glory of them: for it hath been delivered unto me; and to whomsoever I will I give it. If thou therefore wilt worship before me, it shall all be thine. And Jesus answered and said unto him, It is written, Thou shalt worship the Lord thy God, and him only shalt thou serve.—*Luke 4: 1–8*

———————

The interpretation of these symbolical accounts of the Master's moral struggle will be given in the weekly essay. Note today how clearly the record presents the fact that Jesus was harassed by powerful temptations. *Are not great souls most tempted?* Imagine an Australian bushman understanding in even the faintest degree the struggle which Moses faced when he had to decide whether he would enjoy the pleasures of the Egyptian court for a season or bury himself in the desert with the people of God. *You must be built on Moses' scale to know Moses' temptations.* A typhoon cannot operate in a tea-cup. If, therefore, a man is self-complacent, aware of no great battles to fight in his life for God and righteousness, is that a sign of moral nobility or of moral littleness? Temptation is not a disgrace; it is an integral part of manhood's battle: and Jesus was the most tempted of all because he had the greatest powers to control.

And so I live, you see,
Go through the world, try, prove, reject,
Prefer, still struggling to effect
My warfare; happy that I can
Be crossed and thwarted as man,

Not left in God's contempt apart,
With ghastly smooth life, dead at heart....
Thank God, no paradise stands barred
To entry, and I find it hard
To be a Christian, as I said!

☙☙☙

❖ Third Day, Seventh Week

And he led him to Jerusalem, and set him on the pinnacle of the temple, and said unto him, If thou art the Son of God, cast thyself down from hence: for it is written,

He shall give his angels charge concerning thee, to guard thee: and,

On their hands they shall bear thee up,

Lest haply thou dash thy foot against a stone.

And Jesus answering said unto him, It is said, Thou shalt not make trial of the Lord thy God.

And when the devil had completed every temptation, he departed from him for a season.

And Jesus returned in the power of the Spirit into Galilee: and a fame went out concerning him through all the region round about. —*Luke 4: 9–14*

Note especially the closing verse. The Master had gotten out of his temptation new power to fight a larger battle. He made temptation a glorious experience; he was "led up in the Spirit to be tempted," and when he had conquered, he went forth "in the power of the Spirit." *Consider how impossible real nobility of character would be if our goodness were untried innocence instead of victorious virtue. Struggle, built into the fiber of manhood; temptation used as an opportunity for conquest and growth,— this is the Ideal which the Master presents.*

Why comes temptation—but for man to meet
And master, and make crouch beneath his foot,
And so be pedestalled in triumph? Pray
'Lead us into no such temptations, Lord'?

Yea, but, O Thou Whose servants are the bold,
Lead such temptations by the head and hair,
Reluctant dragons, up to who dares fight,
That so he may do battle and have praise!

☙☙☙

❖ Fourth Day, Seventh Week

Our Father who art in heaven, Hallowed be thy name. Thy kingdom come. Thy will be done, as in heaven, so on earth. Give us this day our daily bread. And forgive us our debts, as we also have forgiven our debtors. And bring us not into temptation.—*Matt. 6: 9–13*

Count it all joy, my brethren, when ye fall into manifold temptations; knowing that the proving of your faith worketh patience. And let patience have its perfect work, that ye may be perfect and entire, lacking in nothing.—*James 1: 2–4*

How do you reconcile these two emphases: "Bring us not into temptation" and "Count it all joy when ye fall into manifold temptations"? Some men deliberately seek situations where they know that they are going to be tempted. They wish to test themselves, they say. Is this justifiable? *The man who invites a moral struggle which he could avoid, just for the sake of the moral struggle, is foolishly playing with fire, and he deceives himself, in doing it, into supposing that his motive is good, when in fact it is generally a low curiosity or a morbid desire for new sensations.* We are to avoid temptation wherever we honorably can; but when in the course of positive duty-doing, we *"fall into"* temptation, then we are to go at the task of conquering joyfully, in the spirit which George Macdonald suggests in *Robert Falconer:* "This is a sane, wholesome, practical, working faith: first, that it is a man's business to do the will of God; second, that God takes on himself the special care of that man; and third, that therefore that man ought never to be afraid of anything."

❧❧❧

This is a sane, wholesome, practical, working faith: first, that it is a man's business to do the will of God; second, that God takes on himself the special care of that man; and third, that therefore that man ought never to be afraid of anything.—George Macdonald

❖ Fifth Day, Seventh Week

When the strong man fully armed guardeth his own court, his goods are in peace: but when a stronger than he shall come upon him, and overcome him, he taketh from him his whole armor wherein be trusted, and divideth his spoils. He that is not with me is against me; and he that gathereth not with me scattereth. The unclean spirit when he is gone out of the man, passeth through waterless places, seeking rest, and finding none, he saith, I will turn back unto my house whence I came out. And when he is come, he findeth it swept and garnished. Then goeth he, and taketh to him seven other spirits more evil than himself; and they enter in and dwell there: and the last state of that man becometh worse than the first.—*Luke 11: 21–26*

The truth of this passage is clear; that only by a stronger passion can evil passions be expelled, and that a soul unoccupied by a positive devotion is sure to be occupied by spiritual demons. *The safety of the Master in the presence of temptation lay in his complete and positive devotion to his mission: there was no unoccupied room in his soul where evil could find a home; he knew what Dr. Chalmers called, "The expulsive power of a new affection."* When Ulysses passed the Isle of Sirens, he had himself tied to the mast of the ship, so that he might not yield to the allurement of the sirens' singing—a picture of many a man's pitiful attempts after negative goodness. But when Orpheus passed the Isle of Sirens, he sat on the deck, indifferent, for he too was a musician and could make melody so much more beautiful than the sirens, that their alluring songs were to him discords. Such is the Master's life of positive goodness, so full, so glad, so triumphant, that it conquered sin by surpassing it. Have you such a saving positiveness of loyal devotion in your life?

৵৵৵

The only way to nip sin in the beginning is to resent its attempted entrance into your thoughts.

❖ Sixth Day, Seventh Week

And he said, That which proceedeth out of the man, that defileth the man. For from within, out of the heart of man, evil thoughts proceed, fornications, thefts, murders, adulteries, covetings, wickednesses, deceit, lasciviousness, an evil eye, railing, pride, foolishness: all these evil things proceed from within, and defile the man.—*Mark 7: 20–23*

Ye offspring of vipers, how can ye, being evil, speak good things? for out of the abundance of the heart the mouth speaketh. The good man out of his good treasure bringeth forth good things: and the evil man out of his evil treasure bringeth forth evil things.—*Matt. 12: 34, 35*

Consider the searching truth of these two passages in which the Master insists that the place where temptations must be met and conquered is the realm of secret thinking. These are his commentaries on, "As a man thinketh in his heart, so is he." The evil deeds which we can see, are but the lengthened shadows cast by the real sins which are in the thoughts of men. Consider some of the deeds of which you are most ashamed and trace them back to the wrong habits of thought from which they came. The real war is inward of which the outer action is but the echo and reverberation. *The only way to nip sin in the beginning is to resent its attempted entrance into your* thoughts. *"I will not think it,"* is the end of any special sin, while no man ever yet succeeded in overcoming the impulse to express in action what had been granted habitual right secretly to occupy his mind.

❧❧❧

❖ Seventh Day, Seventh Week

And he goeth up into the mountain, and calleth unto him whom he himself would; and they went unto him. And he appointed twelve, that they might be with him, and that he might send them forth to preach. —*Mark 3: 13, 14*

Now the Lord is the Spirit: and where the Spirit of the Lord is there is liberty. But we all, with unveiled face beholding as in a mirror the glory of the Lord, are transformed into the same image from glory to glory, even as from the Lord the Spirit.—*II Cor. 3: 17, 18*

Think carefully of these two passages. *Character is transformed by the influence of our fellowships. No man can become good merely by trying. A deepening character is generally the unconscious result of consciously chosen influences.* Find a Friend, believe in him and love him; see a great Cause and give yourself to its work; feel the power of a Book and saturate yourself with its spirit; find a Brotherhood of spirits like yours in aspiration and join it; and loving your Friend, serving your Cause, absorbing your Book, and cooperating with your Brotherhood, do not think too much about your own character, for your character will take care of itself. You cannot choose to be Christ-like and attain your choice by trying; but you can choose Christ for your Friend, his Kingdom for your Cause, the Bible for your Book, the Church for your Brotherhood, and these consciously chosen influences will unconsciously transform your life.

❧❧❧

Comment for the Week

The perfection of the Master's character, a perfection so inward and genuine that he did not need to feel ashamed of himself or to shrink from the eye of God, may be at first thought discouraging rather than helpful. The conception lifts him to a remote distance from our own experience and makes the command to imitate him seem an impossible counsel. He clearly made on the first generation of disciples this impression of an inwardly perfect life. They say with John, "There is no unrighteousness in him;" or with Peter, "A lamb without blemish and without spot;" or with the author of the Epistle to the Hebrews, "Holy, harmless, undefiled, separate from sinners." *This impression of perfection which the Master made is entirely unique in the spiritual history of man. No one ever made it before or since, and no one ever tried to claim it.*

Moses was the adored progenitor of the Jewish faith, wherein righteousness was central in the idea of God and the estimate of men, yet he was pictured dying on Nebo's top for his disobedience. Confucius, the revered above all Chinese, and the builder of their religion, says: "In letters I am perhaps equal to other men; but the character of the perfect man, carrying out in his conduct what he professes, is what I have not yet attained to." As for Islam, in the Koran itself Mohammed is commanded to pray pardon for his sins, and God is many times represented as forgiving him. Buddhism is so little a matter of the personality of its founder that no insistence on the perfection of his character is at all discoverable, nor does the affirmation of it hold any importance among his followers. Indeed, not only can no man be discovered who actually did claim the ideal life and make the impression of it; no man can be discovered who ever conceived the thing as possible. If ever you find outside the Christian sphere any mention of sinlessness, it is always accompanied, as in Epictetus, noblest of the Roman teachers, by a statement of its utter impracticability; and Cicero goes so far as to say that no one has ever suggested what a perfect man would be like. Here then in a world where no man, however exalted, ever made the impression of perfection, or ever conceived perfection as a possibility, a man has lived who made people believe that he was living it before their eyes. What sort of character do you estimate it takes to do that?

If this ideal life of the Master is not to discourage rather than inspire us, we must ask whether or not this achievement in character cost a severe moral struggle.

When behind this impression of Jesus' life on others we pierce as far as we can into his own experience, we find, that "The groundtone of his whole self-consciousness is the *undisturbed* sense of communion with God." He held the most exacting idea of goodness ever launched among men. He said that hating was murder, and impure desire adultery; that to harbor a grudge in your heart against an enemy or to be insincere in philanthropy and prayer was real sin. Moreover he must have applied these searching standards mercilessly to his own life. Who was it that told his disciples never to contract the miserable habit of looking for motes in other people's eyes, while beams were in their own? It was Jesus. Who was it that said a man should always take the beam out of his own eye first? It was Jesus. Who was it that laid it down as a fundamental in morals that a man should forgive his fellow, but be so severe with himself as to cut off a hand and cast out an eye for righteousness' sake, if it were needful? It was Jesus. Hard on yourself, easy on others, that was his way. In a word, here was a

Man not only possessing an incomparably spiritual standard of goodness, and a heart exquisitely sensitive to the touch of sin, but urging the unique command to be harder on one's self than on any one else, and yet he seems never to have felt what we mean by moral shame.

Even when he says to the young lawyer, "Why callest thou me good? none is good save one, even God" (Mark 10: 18), he is not revealing shame about himself. Rather he hears the young man superficially bandying compliments about his goodness and he who "learned obedience by the things which he suffered," who was made "perfect through sufferings," who "hath been in all points tempted like as we are, yet without sin" (Heb. 5: 8; 2: 10; 4: 15) turned the youth's too glib ascriptions from himself to God, whose goodness alone is perfect. Jesus' character grew, deepened, struggled with temptation and overcame (Luke 2: 52; Mark 1: 12, 13), but it was always inwardly genuine and right. "The serenity of his vision of God is unclouded, his communion with the Father unbroken; he lives, and everything shows that he lives, in perfect harmony with the divine will."

If this ideal life of the Master is not to discourage rather than inspire us, we must ask whether or not this achievement in character cost a severe moral struggle. If it did not, if he was never searchingly tempted, if his character was untried innocence instead of victorious goodness, tested in the fiery trial of moral struggle, then there is no use in our endeavoring to be like him. *Was Jesus, then, really tempted Did he have in him the capacity for sin? Did he feel the enticement of evil and have inward battles to fight before he could know and do the will of God for him?* The New Testament answers these questions by an unmistakable affirmative: He was "in all points tempted like as we are." But if this is to be real to us, we must study closely the spiritual struggles of the Master.

Great temptations keep company with great powers. The little man fighting his little battles wishes that he were the great man so that the more easily he might overcome them; but when he understands the great man he sees that storms circle around his higher altitudes that make the petty battles of the lower level seem insignificant.

There are three sources of information from which we may expect light on this question. Our own experience may suggest analogies more or less reliable; the disciples who lived with him can surely give us knowledge of the facts; and most of all, Jesus' revelations of his own inward life will be supreme in value. To these three sources we turn, and if they bring a unanimous answer to our question, there can be little room left for doubt.

First, then, our own experience suggests that power is always accompanied by the temptation to misuse it, and that the greater the power, the more self-restraint it requires to use it aright. Great temptations keep company with great powers. The little man fighting his little battles wishes that he were the great man so that the more easily he might overcome them; but when he understands the great man he sees that storms circle around his higher altitudes that make the petty battles of the lower level seem insignificant. The acorn seedling may be impeded by a few dead leaves, but it never will shake in the grip of the tempest until it becomes an oak. The analogy of our experience at once suggests that our Lord was tempted not less but more than we are. Haggard and hungry in the wilderness, as Tintoretto painted him, he was facing temptations that our puny powers can hardly imagine. "If thou art the *Son of God,* command that these stones become bread"; "If thou art the Son of God, cast thyself down": "All the kingdoms of the world... if thou wilt worship me." His masterful powers were met by masterful temptations.

Where does temptation lay its heaviest hand upon us, where we are weak or where we are strong? If a lawyer has no ability to win a difficult case, does he know what it means to have a confessed criminal offer him a hundred thousand dollars to get him clear, or to have a princely fortune dangled before his eyes, tempting him in the legislature to stand on the wrong side of a question for a single hour? Such trials of his moral stamina an incompetent lawyer does not know, but a brilliant pleader knows them well. Temptations always swirl around our powers. Men with attractive social talents are most tempted to convivial dissipation; men with ability to gain wealth face most the danger of money-madness; the collegian with social prestige feels most the temptation to unfraternal exclusiveness. It takes a big country to have a big war. The testimony of our experience is clear that *temptations do not decrease but rather increase with increase of power.*

The Jesus of the gospels lives a real life. He is not mildly inking in a lead-pencil sketch handed down from heaven, but is facing temptations, searching and alluring, from his first desert struggle, to Gethsemane, where surrender to his Father's will cost an inward agony that covered his brow with blood.

If we turn to our second source of information, the testimony of the disciples, we have the analogy of our experience clearly confirmed by their witness. The verisimilitude of the gospels' portrait of Jesus lies largely in this, that while they adore him as the Ideal, they present him to us in the most menial and commonplace situations: they set the background of his life in the poverty-stricken bigoted and sordid social matrix of his day; they invent nothing to heighten the effect of his environment; and amid these mean and ordinary circumstances they show him achieving his character at the cost of a tremendous moral struggle. The Jesus of the gospels lives a real life. He is not mildly inking in a lead-pencil sketch handed down from heaven, but is facing temptations, searching and alluring, from his first desert struggle, to Gethsemane, where surrender to his Father's will cost an inward agony that covered his brow with blood. The words with which Luke's story of the wilderness temptation ends are suggestive: then the devil departed from him *"for a season"* (Luke 4: 13). The Evil One returned many times and the disciples record his coming. They tell us that once Peter started to persuade the Master not to be a suffering Messiah, and that Jesus, like one long hunted by that temptation, turned fiercely on his disciple, saying, "Get thee behind me, Satan! Thou mindest not the things of God!" (Mark 8: 33). The disciples never picture their Master as guarded by an interior prevention from the ability to do wrong. Their comfort in him was that because "He himself hath suffered, being tempted, he is able to succor them that are tempted" (Heb. 2: 18). *His perfection of character does not come from inability to sin, but from ability to conquer.*

Compare the effect of this portrait of our Lord with Tennyson's representation of King Arthur, and the difference is clear. King Arthur's character becomes tiresomely wooden and mechanical; we love the rhythm of the poetry but are wearied by the manufactured perfection of the King. But in the Jesus of the gospels we have moral reality, which is impossible without struggle. If in the end the total impression of his life is one of amazing confidence and peace, it is not the peace of an unruffled pond where no wind blows; but the peace of a planet's orbit where two antagonistic forces have played their parts.

When we seek to understand the nature of the Master's temptation we must turn from the analogy of our experience and the testimony of the disciples to the self-revelation of Jesus. Surely we have his own account of his inward struggle in the story of the temptation in the wilderness. The record of that trial never could have been known unless he had told it. The Master in his account of the three-fold solicitation of the Evil One is dramatizing, in vivid form, after the familiar manner of Ezekiel and Jeremiah, an intense, inward, spiritual struggle. "These are the typical temptations," he seems to say, "which have assailed me, and with which my soul particularly battled when at the beginning I fought out the principles of my ministry in the solitude of the wilderness." Just as the Sermon on the Mount is a sample of the kind of preaching that Jesus continually was doing, so the temptation in the desert is a sample of the kind of moral trial he continually was enduring. If, then, we have here his own account of his temptations, with what eagerness must we turn to study the nature of them!

One element is common to these three typical temptations of the Master: they are all concerned with the use of his unusual power. He had just been baptized. It was one of the crises of his life. His acceptance of the Messiahship, his new consciousness of mastery, his overwhelming sense of divine mission, made it a profound and stirring moment. And, as though the trial of power had a vital connection with the baptism of power, Mark says that "straightway the Spirit driveth him forth into the wilderness to be tempted." *All his temptations were struggles not to misuse his power. The problem of the Master was a problem in self-restraint.*

The marvel of Christ's character lies not alone in what he did, but in what be refrained from doing.

How clear is the spiritual struggle which is pictured by the first temptation, "Command that these stones become bread"! (Matt. 4: 1–4). *The Master was tempted to use his power selfishly.* Consider the powers which were in the Master's possession; think of that ability to inspire devotion, which awakened the envy of Napoleon; measure the actual effect of his personal impact on the world, "lifting empires off their hinges and turning the stream of centuries out of its channel"; and then weigh the meaning of the temptation to use such power selfishly. To be entrusted with billions, and to spend none of it upon yourself, consider the significance of that! The marvel of Christ's character lies not alone in what he did, but in what be refrained from doing. His reserved and utterly unselfish use of his personal endowments; his refusal to turn the hard stones of his experience into the bread of self-satisfaction although he was hungry and was able to work the change, this is our Lord's unexampled masterpiece in the realm of character. He tells us that it cost a hard struggle. He won the battle so completely that we never would have supposed he even was tempted to live a selfish life, unless he had informed us. Now we cannot doubt that all his life, until at the trial he craved not the hard stones of rejection and death but the comfortable bread of release and rest, he was inwardly resisting the desire to use his power for himself. When we imagine what we would have done, had we possessed his endowments; what, indeed, we are doing now, with the endowments that we do possess; we must feel the wonder of the Master's victory over this first great temptation.

The meaning of the second trial in our Lord's life is equally clear. He was tempted to cast himself down from the temple's pinnacle and to expect God to keep him from any harm (Matt. 4: 5–7). Translated into the terms of daily life the significance of this is easily perceived. I was tempted, Jesus seems to say, *presumptuously to demand that God suspend his divine laws to protect me from suffering.*

To undertake the work of saviorhood in a wicked world is always like casting oneself down from a height; it involves suffering and death. But the Master, with his perfect trust in God's illimitable love, with his consciousness that he had been sent by God on a divine mission, was tempted to demand that "angels should bear him up in their hands lest he dash his foot against a stone," that is, to expect immunity from the inevitable consequences of saviorhood. That immunity never came. Not a law of ordinary penalty for great love in an evil world was ever suspended to protect him. He had to drink the cup to its dregs. His life was dashed against the stones.

When Peter suggests that he must not suffer, Jesus feels the pull of the old trial and calls the suggestion Satanic.

Unless the Master himself had told us of this temptation, we might not have suspected its presence in his heart. He paid the price of saviorhood so gladly and fully, he accepted ingratitude and persecution so uncomplainingly, he went to Calvary so fearlessly, that we cannot see from the outside this inward temptation to expect exemption from suffering. But now that he tells us plainly of his struggle, we can feel its presence throughout his life. When Peter suggests that he must not suffer, Jesus feels the pull of the old trial and calls the suggestion Satanic. In Gethsemane be is tempted imperiously to require God to exempt him from the cross. Why must he, the well-beloved Son of God, endure that shame? The agony of that final dealing with his old temptation brings blood to his brow, before he conquers it at last, and says, "Not my will, but thine, be done" (Luke 22: 39–46). When we consider the way we resent the necessity of suffering, even when it comes as the consequence of our own sin, or as part of the ordinary course of human life; when we think further of our unwillingness to endure the suffering that comes from avoidable sacrifice for others, we can understand a little the Master's struggle. But before his victory over it, before his full acceptance of his work of saviorhood with all its consequences, we must stand in inexpressible wonder.

The third typical temptation of the Master is suited only to the powers of a supremely great personality. I was shown all the kingdoms of the world, Jesus seems to say, and was offered them, if I would adopt Satanic means to get them. *I was tempted to substitute a temporal kingdom for an internal, spiritual empire (Matt. 4: 8–10).*

We have no abilities to which such a temptation could appeal. We can grasp it only in imagination. But if we can think of ourselves as possessing such endowments as belonged to our Lord, to which Christendom today bears impressive witness, we can guess something of the force of this temptation. The Messianic expectations of his people cried to him for a

Kingdom, of righteousness, to be sure, but external, material, founded, if need be, on force. The people offering him a crown begged him to yield to the solicitations of the tempter (John 6: 15). Peter at Caesarea Philippi rebuked him for resisting longer the opportunity, and during the last week at Jerusalem the aroused and dangerous hopes of the multitude persuaded Caiaphas that Jesus must die or be the center of a revolution (John 11: 47–50). That it cost the Master an inward struggle to surrender all thought of earthly empire, we never could have suspected unless he had told us. Even when the crucifixion was the alternative, he resisted the solicitations of the tempter with such absolute finality that were it not for his account of the wilderness experience, we never could guess that he had even thought of an external kingdom.

To be gifted with supernal powers and never to use them selfishly; to be sent on a divine mission and never to expect God to stop the lions' mouths; to be offered a temporal kingdom and to be crucified for a spiritual one, that was the temptation and triumph of Jesus. He was tempted in all points like as we are, but we never have been tempted as he was. A man would have to be built on Christ's scale to face his moral trials. On the glistening summit where he lived, there were gales in which we never could have stood; they would have blown us off!

❧❧❧

Notes

8

The Master's Fearlessness

Many men take as a matter of course the social and industrial conditions of the generation into which they are born. If slavery is extant, or child-labor, or a seven-day week for workers in their mills they look upon these things as the rules of the game. They do not ask how long the conditions have existed, whether they are right, how long they ought to stay; they simply accept the rules as existing and play the game as hard as they can. Note that Jesus would not take for granted any condition that seemed to him wrong, no matter of how long standing or of how great authority. He believed in the Kingdom of God which is coming, and to accord with which all present conditions must be changed.

Daily Readings

❖ **First Day, Eighth Week**

And he departed thence, and went into their synagogue: and behold, a man having a withered hand. And they asked him, saying, is it lawful to heal on the sabbath day? that they might accuse him. And he said unto them, What man shall there be of you, that shall have one sheep, and if this fall into a pit on the sabbath day, will be not lay hold on it, and lift it out? How much then is a man of more value than a sheep! Wherefore it is lawful to do good on the sabbath day. Then saith he to the man, Stretch forth thy hand. And he stretched it forth; and it was restored whole, as the other. But the Pharisees went out, and took counsel against him, how they might destroy him.—*Matt. 12: 9–14*

Consider how a man who lives up to his best always has to run counter to many of the established customs of his day. Jesus, for example, was living an ideal life in an unideal world, and a clash was inevitable. In today's passage the clash is between his love of men and the customary

Sabbath laws. Broaden the application of the truth behind this special disagreement, and consider how certain it is that any man who lives a really Christlike life will have to meet the hostility of many ordinary customs in business, in society, in college. *Are you living a life that is on the average plane, doing what everybody else does, drifting with the current, or are you following your best ideals enough so that you definitely clash with some of the unworthy habits in the social life about you?* Think over the points of conflict.

❧❧❧

❖ Second Day, Eighth Week

Then there come to Jesus from Jerusalem Pharisees and scribes, saying, Why do thy disciples transgress the tradition of the elders? for they wash not their hands when they eat bread. And he answered and said unto them, Why do ye also transgress the commandment of God because of your tradition? For God said, Honor thy father and thy mother: and, He that speaketh evil of father or mother, let him die the death. But ye say, Whosoever shall say to his father or his mother, That wherewith thou mightest have been profited by me is given to God; he shall not honor his father. And ye have made void the word of God because of your tradition.—*Matt. 15: 1–6*

Consider again how constantly the Master is compelled to stand out against the customs of his people. The drag of ordinary standards is always down, whenever a man tries to live his best life. In a democracy, we are tempted to think that "The voice of the people is the voice of God." Is that true? Which would win by a popular vote: Wagner or ragtime? Shakespeare or vaudeville? George Eliot or sensational fiction? The finest ideals of character or the mediocre? *The world is not yet saved, and it always pulls down on the best in us. Any man who is going to achieve worthy character must have the power and courage to stand out against debasing, vulgar standards.* Think of the truth of this in regard to habits of conversation in your circle; in regard to social customs, especially where young men and women are concerned; in regard to the character of fiction often popular; in regard to flippancy and irreverence about religion.

❧❧❧

❖ Third Day, Eighth Week

And it came to pass, that he was going on the sabbath day through the grainfields; and his disciples began, as they went, to pluck the ears. And the Pharisees said unto him, Behold, why do they on the sabbath day that which is not lawful? And he said unto them, Did ye never read what David did, when he had need, and was hungry, he, and they that were with him? How he entered into the house of God when Abiathar was high priest, and ate the showbread, which it is not lawful to eat save for the priests, and gave also to them that were with him? And he said unto them, The sabbath was made for man, and not man for the sabbath: so that the Son of man is lord even of the sabbath.—*Mark 2: 23–28*

Note once more with what kindness but with what uncompromising firmness, the Master refused to subject himself to the dead level of the habits of his people. It takes the deepest courage to maintain this attitude in the face of the misunderstanding and criticism that inevitably come. With Jesus it meant, in the end, death; with us it means often ostracism, loss of friends, or a reputation for eccentricity or prudishness. Is it not true, however, that in the long run the one who with kindly insistence, lives up to his best is most respected by those whose respect counts? And is it not true that the only way society is improved is by those who dare to live in advance of the customs of their time? *Will your college, your town, your church be better, because you have been willing without ostentation, without condescension, but with uncompromising good-will, to live above the average level?*

 махмахмах

❖ Fourth Day, Eighth Week

And he called to him the multitude again, and said unto them, Hear me all of you, and understand: there is nothing from without the man, that going into him can defile him; but the things which proceed out of the man are those that defile the man. And when he was entered into the house from the multitude, his disciples asked of him the parable. And he saith unto them, Are ye so without understanding also? Perceive ye not, that whatsoever from without goeth into the man, it cannot defile him.... This he said, making all meats clean. And he said, That which proceedeth out of the man, that defileth the man.—*Mark 7: 14–20*

In the midst of a religious system, blighted by ceremonialism, Jesus was earnestly laboring for a better type of spiritual life and for a nobler sort of religious thought. *He never took for granted the existing situation; he believed in something better yet to come; and he threw himself into the Cause of the Future.* What is the religious situation in your college or community? Are you taking it for granted? Are you saying that it always has been and always will be that way? Are you merely standing over against the situation and criticizing it? Then catch the Master's spirit. The religious conditions in any social group can be radically changed, often by one person, who is wise, friendly, persistent, fearless, and who has faith in the better day yet to come, for which he works. Such a person will often meet with opposition, but is not this desire to better the religious life of your college or town, and this willingness to try, in however small a way to help, part of your discipleship to Jesus?

❧❧❧

❖ Fifth Day, Eighth Week

And the multitudes that went before him, and that followed, cried, saying, Hosanna to the son of David: Blessed is he that cometh in the name of the Lord; Hosanna in the highest. And when he was come into Jerusalem, all the city was stirred, saying, Who is this? And the multitudes said, This is the prophet, Jesus, from Nazareth of Galilee.

And Jesus entered into the temple of God, and cast out all them that sold and bought in the temple, and overthrew the tables of the money-changers, and the seats of them that sold the doves; and he saith unto them, It is written, My house shall be called a house of prayer: but ye make it a den of robbers.—*Matt. 21: 9–13*

Many men take as a matter of course the social and industrial conditions of the generation into which they are born. If slavery is extant, or child-labor, or a seven-day week for workers in their mills they look upon these things as the rules of the game. They do not ask how long the conditions have existed, whether they are right, how long they ought to stay; they simply accept the rules as existing and play the game as hard as they can. *Note that Jesus would not take for granted any condition that seemed to him wrong, no matter of how long standing or of how great authority. He believed in the Kingdom of God which is coming, and to accord with which all present conditions must be changed.* Do you share this faith in the social future of the race, and are you going to be one of the forward-looking, fearless men of your generation, who has "tasted the powers of the age to come"?

❧❧❧

❖ Sixth Day, Eighth Week

Then cometh Jesus from Galilee to the Jordan unto John, to be baptized of him. But John would have hindered him, saying, I have need to be baptized of thee, and comest thou to me? But Jesus answering said unto him, Suffer it now: for thus it becometh us to fulfil all righteousness. Then he suffereth him. And Jesus, when he was baptized, went up straightway from the water: and lo, the heavens were opened unto him, and he saw the Spirit of God descending as a dove, and coming upon him; and lo, a voice out of the heavens, saying, This is my beloved Son, in whom I am well pleased.—*Matt. 3: 13–17*

This self-dedication of the Master was full of beauty at its beginning, as the consciousness of his great mission came upon him, but think of the self-denial that it was going to involve and the courage that it was going to require for its fulfilment. *Are you fearless enough to put yourself absolutely in the hands of God to be used anywhere as he wills, regardless of the cost?* This is the central act of moral courage upon which all else depends.

> Laid on Thine altar, O my Lord divine,
>> Accept this gift today, for Jesus' sake:
> I have no jewels to adorn Thy shrine,
>> No far-famed sacrifice to make;
> But here within my trembling hand I bring
>> This will of mine—a thing that seemeth small,
> But Thou alone, O Lord, canst understand
>> How when I yield Thee this, I yield mine all.

ô≈ ô≈ ô≈

❖ Seventh Day, Eighth Week

In the mean time, when the many thousands of the multitude were gathered together, insomuch that they trod one upon another, he began to say unto his disciples first of all, Beware ye of the leaven of the Pharisees, which is hypocrisy. But there is nothing covered up, that shall not be revealed; and hid, that shall not be known. Wherefore whatsoever ye have said in the darkness shall be heard in the light; and what ye have spoken in the ear in the inner chambers shall be proclaimed upon the housetops. And I say unto you my friends, Be not afraid of them that kill the body, and after that have no more that they can do.—*Luke 12: 1–4*

Note that Jesus' fearlessness is here intimately associated with his confident faith that evil cannot win, but that rather the quiet beginnings of good shall in the end be public and universal. He knew that working with God and righteousness, he was on the winning side, whatever the immediate opposition. Have you this same faith undergirding your life? Do you believe deeply that God's Cause is going to win, that evil is beaten in advance, that in all our labor for righteousness we are building roadways over which the forces of good shall some day celebrate a triumph? *Think how the faith of far-seeing men that slavery could be abolished necessarily preceded its abolishment; and consider the need today for men who really are confident that war can be done away, that industrial injustice and political corruption can be stopped, that the brotherhood of man is a possibility, and that the world can be Christianized.*

ô≈ ô≈ ô≈

Comment for the Week

Emerson describes a hero as one who, "Taking both reputation and life in his hand, will, with perfect urbanity, dare the gibbet and the mob, by the absolute truth of his speech and rectitude of his behavior." That the Master had need of this sort of heroism and that to the last full measure of devotion he paid the price which such heroism costs, is a commonplace; but we do not perceive the full meaning of this generality until we enter by sympathetic understanding into the concrete problems which he actually faced.

When we hear the Master say, *"Be not afraid of them that kill the body, and after that have no more that they can do"* (Luke 12: 4), we may be sure that these words are a revelation of his own life's problem. From the first, the nature of his message and the method of his work outraged the orthodox and pious people of his generation. He had to keep his soul free from all fear of mortal clay, or he never could have continued his mission. He preached a gospel that to the Jews seemed revolutionary. When the people heard him speak they cried, "What is this? a new teaching!" (Mark 1: 27). As they watched his marvellous ministry to folk of all castes, they said, "We never saw it on this fashion" (Mark 2: 12). So novel, so uncomfortably revolutionary were the nature and method of Jesus' mission that the question "Why?" followed him like his own shadow; "Why do ye eat and drink with the publicans?" (Luke 5: 30); "Why walk not thy disciples according to the tradition of the elders?" (Mark 7: 5). He was a disturbing personality to the religious leaders of his people. He, an "unlicensed practitioner," interpreted the law in new and startling ways; he discounted precise commands in the code, like the Mosaic allowance of divorce, by general principles, which, he said, proved the precise commands to be temporary, not permanent (Mark 10: 1–9); he disregarded established conventionalities; he upbraided the Rabbis, and referring to time-honored corollaries of the law, he deliberately said, "Ye have made void the word of God because of your tradition" (Matt. 15: 6). He seemed to the Jews a dangerous revolutionary in society, and in religion an innovator.

Now the Pharisees, and behind them, the great body of the Jews, over whom the Pharisaic influence was dominant, were devoted with sincere and zealous earnestness to the protection of the Law. The Law, whether in the writings of the Old Testament or in the oral traditions which, as they thought, simply made explicit what the Old Testament meant, was to them the express will of God. Therefore, whether in a great matter like the sacredness of a human life, or in a small matter like avoiding the eating of an egg laid on the Sabbath, they were equally devout and careful. When the

Roman, Petronius, proposed an imperial statue in the temple area, the answer of the Pharisees was resolute and final; "We shall die rather than transgress the Law." During the Maccabean wars, thousands of pious Jewish soldiers had allowed themselves to be cut to pieces on the Sabbath, rather than break the Law by fighting. Seldom, if ever, in religious history has there been an example of orthodoxy more solid, compact and passionately conscientious. When the mob gathered during Passover week, to cry "Crucify him," we are told that they would not make themselves ceremonially unclean by stepping into the area of Pilate's court (John 18: 28). They lined up just outside the curb, examples of scrupulous devotion to their duty as they understood it, and cried out for the death of the Son of man. *In the ears of people so zealous for their ancient Law, imagine how hatefully novel and revolutionary sounded the voice that said, "It was said unto you of old time, but I say unto you."*

As Beethoven was an innovator in music, who first had mastered, to a degree no other man of his generation equaled, the musical accomplishments of the past, so our Lord was reverent toward the Law and the prophets, understood them, loved them and felt the meaning of them, in a way that no Pharisee could surpass.

No one ever yet attacked points of view which had been thus accepted as truth for many years, which had been built into systems of thought, strengthened by social customs and made precious by long association, without meeting the bitterest hostility. The rancor of the established order fell upon Jesus the innovator, and it was all the more merciless because, as the Master himself said, they thought that they were offering service unto God (John 16: 2). To bring new ideas in science such as revolutionize the thoughts of men about the physical world, the origin and history of life, always has meant questioning, reviling, persecution and sometimes death. But to bring new ideas in religion, when the most sacred sentiments have twined themselves about the old; to suggest new conceptions of God, when the old have been homes for the soul, how holy has hatred against the innovator seemed in such a case! For new ideas like those of the Master cannot be added to the former stock, as one more shot is dropped into a bag. They come rather as fresh elements in a chemical compound that compel a readjustment of the whole. The entire formula shifts when they arrive. Such was the effect of Jesus' truth, and inevitably he bore the brunt of hatred for it.

We need to balance our thought of Jesus as a revolutionist in religion, by noting that he always thought of himself as one who was fulfilling, not destroying, the old revelation of God to Israel. His complaint against the traditions of the elders was that they spoiled and obscured the real meaning of the Law (Mark 7: 8). The Old Testament for Jesus was summed up in love for God and man: on that "the whole law hangeth, and the prophets" (Matt. 22: 40). Jesus said, I came not to destroy this spiritual meaning, but to fulfil it (see Matt. 5: 17). As Beethoven was an innovator in music, who first had mastered, to a degree no other man of his generation equaled, the musical accomplishments of the past, so our Lord was reverent toward the Law and the prophets, understood them, loved them and felt the meaning of them, in a way that no Pharisee could surpass. His originality was rooted in the past, and drew from it the very sap that made the fresh growth possible. He saw his "new teaching" as the fulfilment of the old teaching, not a jot or tittle of which should pass away (Matt. 5: 18). He thought of himself as bringing in the noon of which the former truth was the dawn. But like all heralds of new light he met the hatred of the obscurantists. As eyes, accustomed to twilight, shut themselves instinctively against a stronger sun, so the Jews closed their souls against the Gospel. It seemed to them not fulfilment but destruction. As Jesus put it in a figure with a play of humor in it, *"No man having drunk old wine desireth new; for he saith, The old is good"* (Luke 5: 39).

In the crises of life, when we have no time for long premeditation, our words show where our souls have been feeding.

The deep reverence of the Master for the truth which the prophets proclaimed is manifested in many indirect ways. Twice he is represented as repeating a word of Hosea: "I desire mercy, and not sacrifice" (Matt. 9: 13; 12: 7). When he faces the hypocrisy of the Pharisees, he instinctively expresses his feeling in the language of Isaiah:

This people honoreth me with their lips,
But their heart is far from me

(Mark 7: 6). In the crises of life, when we have no time for long premeditation, our words show where our souls have been feeding. Consider what it means then that in the stress of temptation the Master announces his decisive refusal of the tempter in scriptural words (Matt. 4: 4, 7–10); that when in indignation he clears the temple of its profaners, he cries, from Isaiah, "My house shall be called a house of prayer," and then, with a quick transition to Jeremiah adds, "Ye make it a den of robbers" (Matt. 21: 13); that in the agony of the crucifixion he turns to the Psalms for expression of his anguish and his trust, "My God, my God, why hast thou forsaken me?" (Matt. 27: 46); "Father, into thy hands I commend my spirit" (Luke 23: 46). The Master's mind was saturated with the Old Testament. If he was a revolutionary force in the religious life of his people, it was not because he thought less than they thought of the ancient prophets. He cries that the

Pharisees are like their fathers; they slay the prophets and then decorate their tombs in formal and meaningless respect (Matt. 23: 29–31). They have not caught the prophets' spirit, nor seen, as the prophets saw, that God is a living God who has never said his last word on any subject, but always, with more things to tell us than we now can bear (John 16: 12), endeavors to fulfil old revelations with new. "Every scribe," said Jesus, "who hath been made a disciple to the kingdom of heaven is like unto a man that is a householder, who bringeth forth out of his treasure things new and old" (Matt. 13: 52).

We need also to balance our thought of Jesus as a revolutionist in religion by noting that he did his best to adapt his new truth to the understanding of his people and to make it easy for them to accept it. Brought up in the observance of the Jewish Law, he always was faithful to it, to the limit of his conscience's allowance, and the same attitude he urged on his disciples. "The scribes and the Pharisees," he said, "sit on Moses' seat: all things therefore whatsoever they bid you, these do and observe" (Matt. 23: 2). When he berated the Pharisees for tithing mint, anise and cummin, and neglecting the weightier matters of the Law, he did not entirely rule out the tithing. Justice, mercy and faith might have been served, he said, and the other things not left undone (Matt. 23: 23). When he compared a temple sacrifice with brotherliness, to the detriment of the former, he still added, "Then come and offer thy gift" (Matt. 5: 23, 24), and when he healed a leper, he told him, according to the Jewish Law, to show himself to the priest (Matt. 8: 4).

> **With no motive for persisting save his sense of duty, he walked straight toward the cross, although compromise, equivocation, mental reservation, even simple silence would have saved him; and at last with a mob howling for his crucifixion he stood his ground without hedging, without hesitation and without fear.**

Plainly the Master was endeavoring to fulfil his mission as peaceably as possible. He scrupulously worked within the boundaries of their synagogues; he used ancient and honored terms, "Kingdom of God," "Son of Man," "Messiah"; when he did transgress laws, such as guarded the Sabbath day, he tried to mediate his new position by arguments that the Jews could understand. He said that David in an emergency broke technical Sabbath laws; why not he? (Mark 2: 25–28). He said that according to their laws a poor man could take an ox from a pit on the Sabbath day; why might he not heal a man? (Luke 13: 15, 16; 14: 1–6). With surprising patience he tried to make the ascent from their level to his, gradual and easy. He wanted not to destroy, but to fulfil.

When, however, his reverence for the old Law and his endeavor peaceably to mediate the new truth were unappreciated and the Pharisees forced the conflict, he was uncompromising and fearless. If they would have it so he had come "not to send peace, but a sword" (Matt 10: 34). Here was the immediate reason for his life of suffering, abuse and martyrdom: he "would not hesitate, he would not equivocate, he would not retreat a single inch, and he would be heard." Many kinds of courage deserve the admiration of men: the physical courage that causes a cavalry captain to marshal his men for an obviously fatal charge and to ride down the hesitating ranks, crying, "Men, what is the matter with you? Do you want to live forever?" the courage of steadfast loyalty that causes a Protestant woman, tied to the stake, with the fagots beginning to burn, to refuse recantation, although her babe, held just out of reach, weeps for her embrace, and the torturer cries, "Abjure! Abjure!" But the courage of the Master includes this and more. He took a new truth, needed by the world, and proclaiming it kindly was met by bitter antagonism; he saw the multitudes dwindle as he proclaimed it, from hundreds to scores, from scores to a dozen, and saw even these uncertain in their allegiance; he found the organized religion of his day bent on his destruction and yet, with no motive for persisting save his sense of duty, he walked straight toward the cross, although compromise, equivocation, mental reservation, even simple silence would have saved him; and at last with a mob howling for his crucifixion he stood his ground without hedging, without hesitation and without fear. One phrase continually upon the Master's lips is a true revelation of his spirit: "Fear not" (Matt. 10: 26–31; Luke 12: 4–32).

In two special ways the fearlessness of the Master is revealed in his dealing with the organized religion of his day. *First, he persisted in making a man's relationship with God depend on spiritual, not ceremonial conditions.* The Rabbis had interpreted the requirements of God as not only moral but ritual. To eat with unwashed hands was a ritual sin, and a Rabbi who dared deny it was excommunicated and buried in unhallowed ground. It is easy to be unjust to the Pharisees in this regard, for it must always be remembered that their passion for the whole Law, both moral and ceremonial, was a zealous desire to do the will of God to the most minute details. We must not forget that it was a Jewish lawyer who suggested that beautiful summary of the Law as love to God and neighbor, to which the Master gave his hearty approval. Nevertheless, while it is easy to see the reasonableness of the Pharisees' attitude when their premises are granted, it is clear also that tithing mint, anise and cummin, and neglecting the weightier matters of the Law, justice and mercy and faith, has always been the inevitable result of making man's relationship with God depend on ceremonial. The Talmud contains refinements of the rabbinical law absurd in their pettiness, refinements the like of which were doubtless in force in Jesus' day. On the Sabbath if a man were to pull out a feather from the wing of a bird, cut off the top and pluck off the fluff below, he would commit three sins, involving three sin offerings; and the weighty commandment was even laid down that on the Sabbath, a ladder could not be carried from one pigeon roost to another, but without lifting it from the ground, could be *leaned* from one to another.

Against the idea of religious living here represented the Master resolutely took his stand. He broke the Sabbath laws himself and led his disciples to, both by plucking corn in the fields and eating it, and by doing works of mercy (Matt. 12: 1ff; Mark 3: 1ff). He utterly spurned the requirements about clean and unclean foods (Mark 7: 14–19). He would not fast according to the Jewish schedule, and represented a penitent Publican as in a better spiritual estate than a law-abiding Pharisee who fasted twice in a week and gave tithes of all that he possessed (Luke 18: 9–14). To show that he understood well the purport of his attitude, he told the Jews that he would not sew his truth as a patch on their old system nor put his new wine into their old wineskins (Luke 5: 36–39). He was rather making a new garment altogether, and was putting the spirit of his new truth into new forms. Can there be any doubt of the inevitable issue of such fearless radicalism, when it faces the organized system of a self-complacent church? Mark tells us that after the first sample of Jesus' attitude toward their Sabbath laws, "The Pharisees went out, and straightway with the Herodians took counsel against him, how they might destroy him" (Mark 3: 6).

When we consider the courage which the Master's life required, and the way in which he met the demand without wavering, we are not surprised to catch in Peter, years afterward, an echo of that same spirit. "But even if ye should suffer for righteousness' sake," says the apostle, "blessed are ye: and fear not their fear, neither be troubled."

The same fearless attitude characterized the Master in his dealing with the narrow exclusiveness of the Pharisees. According to the orthodox opinion of the day, none could stand in God's favor save pious, law-abiding Israelites. Even the multitude of Jews who had no time to learn or, by the conditions of their work, were prevented from practising the minutiae of the Law, were accursed (John 7: 49). The neighboring Samaritans were so under the ban of Jewish contempt, that no orthodox Rabbi would step on Samaritan soil, and when the Jews sought a word of opprobrium, to apply to Jesus, comparable to saying that he had a devil, they called him a Samaritan (John 8: 48). Against this provincialism the

Master openly took up the battle. When he preached his first sermon in his home town, he aroused an antagonism that nearly issued in his death, by telling them that, with plenty of widows in Israel in the time of Elijah, God had favored a widow of heathen Sidon, by sending the prophet to her; that, with many lepers in Israel in the time of Elisha, God had favored the Syrian, Naaman, by healing him (Luke 4: 16–30). He told his audiences of scribes and Pharisees that God would welcome to his feast the Gentiles, because the Jews had not accepted his invitation (Matt. 8: 11, 12); and, as for the outcasts of Israel, he put his truth in a most excoriating form: "The publicans and the harlots go into the kingdom of God before you" (Matt. 21: 31). When the inevitable issue was at hand, to which such fearless truth-telling always leads, if it smites a self-complacent orthodoxy and a proud exclusiveness, the Master did not flinch. He said, with cutting irony, that it could not be that a prophet could perish out of the Holy City (Luke 13: 33), and knowing the end, he "steadfastly set his face to go to Jerusalem" (Luke 9: 51). Once within the city, the headquarters of his enemies, he threw down the gauntlet by clearing the Temple of their thieving henchmen. When a deputation from the Sanhedrin conferred with him about his action, he told them the scathing story of the vineyard keepers who maltreated the messengers of the owner and now were planning to slay the owner's son. In words that are at once an appeal and an accusation he ends his parable, "The kingdom of God shall be taken away from you, and shall be given to a nation bringing forth the fruits thereof" (Matt. 21: 33–46). Such fearlessness under such conditions can have but a single end, and to that end the Master went with utter steadfastness, saying, even when he staggered under the weight of his cross, "Weep not for me, but weep for yourselves" (Luke 23: 28).

When we consider the courage which the Master's life required, and the way in which he met the demand without wavering, we are not surprised to catch in Peter, years afterward, an echo of that same spirit. "But even if ye should suffer for righteousness' sake," says the apostle, "blessed are ye: and fear not their fear, neither be troubled" (I Peter 3: 14). We are acquainted with the familiar petition of the prayer-meeting, asking God for the presence in our lives of those gentle and lovable qualities which shall remind people that we have been with Jesus. Such petitions may well be offered, but the characteristics of the disciples which in that first generation most reminded men of Jesus were not the passive but the active virtues, not gentleness but fearlessness. *"Now when they beheld the boldness of Peter and John," we read, "they took knowledge of them, that they had been with Jesus"* (Acts 4: 13)

ह ह ह

Notes

9

The Master's Affection

Everywhere he leaves the impression of affectionate good-will, not scattered and diffuse, comprehending all men in a vague generosity of sentiment, but concrete and particular, seeking special men and women for its objects. In a cross section of his prayer, when alone upon the hillside he communed with God, one would surely have found individual names— some blind Bartimaeus, some child he had met yesterday, and especially the inner circle of his friends. If the field was the world, as he said, the Master's immediate personal relationships were the gardens where the plants of kindness and goodwill were prepared for transplanting to the larger soil.

Daily Readings

❖ First Day, Ninth Week

Even as the Father hath loved me, I also have loved you: abide ye in my love. If ye keep my commandments, ye shall abide in my love; even as I have kept my Father's commandments, and abide in his love. These things have I spoken unto you, that my joy may be in you, and that your joy may be made full. This is my commandment, that ye love one another, even as I have loved you. Greater love hath no man than this, that a man lay down his life for his friends. Ye are my friends, if ye do the things which I command you. No longer do I call you servants; for the servant knoweth not what his lord doeth: but I have called you friends; for all things that I heard from my Father I have made known unto you.—*John 15: 9–15*

No one of the earlier gospels contains so beautiful an expression of affectionate friendliness as this, but, as we shall see, they do present the Master as one who must have felt toward his disciples the most tender and constant love. *Consider the difficult combination in Jesus' character between his heroic and revolutionary fearlessness, his capacity for indignation on the one side, and on the other this deep, friendly tenderness.* We feel a like wonder when we turn from Paul's splendid statesmanship, his amazing power of intellectual grasp, and his dauntless courage to read a passage like this: "We were gentle in the midst of you, as when a nurse cherisheth her own children: even so, being affectionately desirous of you, we were well pleased to impart unto you, not the gospel of God only, but also our own souls, because ye were become very dear to us" (I Thess. 2: 7, 8). Some men are ashamed of such a deep and moving affection in friendship, but they are the small men. *The great men are always the gentle men.*

ॐॐॐ

❖ Second Day, Ninth Week

In that hour came the disciples unto Jesus, saying, Who then is greatest in the kingdom of heaven? And he called to him a little child, and set him in the midst of them, and said, Verily I say unto you, Except ye turn, and become as little children, ye shall in no wise enter into the kingdom of heaven. Whosoever therefore shall humble himself as this little child, the same is the greatest in the kingdom of heaven. And whoso shall receive one such little child in my name receiveth me: but whoso shall cause one of these little ones that believe on me to stumble, it is profitable for him that a great millstone should be hanged about his neck, and that he should be sunk in the depth of the sea.

See that ye despise not one of these little ones: for I say unto you, that in heaven their angels do always behold the face of my Father who is in heaven. How think ye? if any man have a hundred sheep, and one of them be gone astray, doth he not leave the ninety and nine, and go unto the mountains, and seek that which goeth astray? And if so be that he find it, verily I say unto you, he rejoiceth over it more than over the ninety and nine which have not gone astray. Even so it is not the will of your Father who is in heaven, that one of these little ones should perish.—*Matt. 18: 1– 6; 10–14*

_____

We are going to note in this week's study that the Master's teaching is always family teaching. *Consider today that in just one social group is each individual of boundless value, no matter how many individuals there are. That group is the true family.* See in today's passage how the Master carries this family idea out to the whole race and applies it even to little children. He thinks of humanity as a family with one Father, and each member of it of infinite value. How great must be the capacity for love in one who can really take the race into his affection as though all men were members of his own household and not one of them negligible. Consider yourself as living in such a human family and regarded, with such love as the Master's, by the Father of all. Is your life a worthy response to such love? Are you living as though you were of infinite value in the sight of God? And are you living as though all other people, even forgotten "little ones," were of infinite value too? *Think now of some neglected, ostracized, unbefriended person and begin today to treat him especially as though he were valuable to you.*

ತ್ರಿ-ತ್ರಿ-ತ್ರಿ

❖ Third Day, Ninth Week

And the son said unto him, Father, I have sinned against heaven, and in thy sight: I am no more worthy to be called thy son. But the father said to his servants, Bring forth quickly the best robe, and put it on him; and put a ring on his hand, and shoes on his feet: and bring the fatted calf, and kill it, and let us eat, and make merry: for this my son was dead, and is alive again; he was lost, and is found. And they began to be merry. Now his elder son was in the field: and as he came and drew nigh to the house, he heard music and dancing. And he called to him one of the servants, and inquired what these things might be. And he said unto him, Thy brother is come; and thy father hath killed the fatted calf, because he hath received him safe and sound. But he was angry, and would not go in: and his father came out, and entreated him. But he answered and said to his father, Lo, these many years do I serve thee, and I never transgressed a commandment of thine; and yet thou never gavest me a kid, that I might make merry with my friends: but when this thy son came, who hath devoured thy living with harlots, thou killedst for him the fatted calf. And he said unto him, Son, thou art ever with me, and all that is mine is thine. But it was meet to make merry and be glad: for this thy brother was dead, and is alive again; and was lost, and is found.—*Luke 15: 21–32*

Do not be content with reading the closing portion of the parable of the Lost Son; read it all. See how clearly here the Master puts his Gospel into family terms. *In only one social group, a true family, are relationships indissoluble, so that a bad son is still a son, an unfaithful brother is still a brother.* The Master applied this family principle to all life. The Pharisees, he said, were denying the relationship of brotherhood with sinners, just as the elder brother did with the prodigal, whereas all men are our brothers, often wicked, ignorant, corrupt, but still our brothers. Think what it would mean to have the Master's principle accepted, and brotherhood and sisterhood recognized with all human beings. Think of changes that would have to be made in our business and industrial life. Think of the deepening motive for social service and missions. *Think of the changes that would come in your personal attitude toward some particular people.*

࿇࿇࿇

❖ **Fourth Day, Ninth Week**

And the apostles gather themselves together unto Jesus; and they told him all things, whatsoever they had done, and whatsoever they had taught. And he saith unto them, Come ye yourselves apart into a desert place, and rest awhile. For there were many coming and going, and they had no leisure so much as to eat. And they went away in the boat to a desert place apart. And the people saw them going, and many knew them, and they ran together there on foot from all the cities, and outwent them. And he came forth and saw a great multitude, and he had compassion on them, because they were as sheep not having a shepherd: and he began to teach them many things.—*Mark 6: 30–34*

O Jerusalem, Jerusalem, that killeth the prophets, and stoneth them that are sent unto her! How often would I have gathered thy children together, even as a hen gathereth her chickens under her wings, and ye would not! Behold, your house is left unto you desolate.—*Matt. 23: 37, 38*

We have been thinking of the family idea behind Jesus' love for men: that God is our Father, that all we are brethren; that as in a home, each individual is of infinite value, and that the relationships of fatherhood, sonship and brotherhood are indissoluble, so that no man's sin can utterly free me from being brother to him as much as I can. *Let today's Scripture make you feel how these basal ideas of the Master were in his life warmed and made effective by a deep, compassionate, overflowing love for men.* You hold the Christian theory of fatherhood and brotherhood: has it become real in your daily attitude and feeling toward men?

࿇࿇࿇

❖ **Fifth Day, Ninth Week**

Now before the feast of the passover, Jesus knowing that his hour was come that he should depart out of this world unto the Father, having loved his own that were in the world, he loved them unto the end. And during supper, the devil having already put into the heart of Judas Iscariot, Simon's son, to betray him, Jesus, knowing that the Father had given all things into his hands, and that he came forth from God, and goeth unto God, riseth from supper, and layeth aside his garments; and he took a towel, and girded himself. Then he poureth water into the basin, and began to wash the disciples' feet, and to wipe them with the towel wherewith he was girded.

So when he had washed their feet, and taken his garments and sat down again, he said unto them, Know ye what I have done to you? Ye call me, Teacher, and Lord: and ye say well; for so I am. If I then, the Lord and the Teacher, have washed your feet, ye also ought to wash one another's feet. For I have given you an example, that ye also should do as I have done to you.—*John 13: 1–5; 12–15*

Could there be, under the circumstances, a more moving expression of deep friendship than this? Friendship is of many qualities. Addison says:

The friendships of the world are oft
> *Confederacies in vice or leagues of pleasure;*
Ours has severest virtue for its basis
> And such friendship ends not but with life.

Friendship is like a plant that grows in all zones, nipped and wizened in the north, luxuriant and beautiful in the south. Consider the friendship of the Master and his disciples, how it was nurtured by a common faith, a common hope, a common devotion to the same Cause; how it grew in a climate of spiritual sympathy and mutual service. *Jesus was friendly to everybody but he could be friends only with those who consented to meet him on his own high terms: "Ye are my friends, if ye do whatsoever I command you." Do your friendships partake of this high quality, and are you thus a member of the circle of the Friends of the Master?*

෨෨෨

❖ Sixth Day, Ninth Week

That which was from the beginning, that which we have heard, that which we have seen with our eyes, that which we beheld, and our hands handled, concerning the Word of life (and the life was manifested, and we have seen, and bear witness, and declare unto you the life, the eternal life, which was with the Father, and was manifested unto us); that which we have seen and heard declare we unto you also, that ye also may have fellowship with us: yea, and our fellowship is with the Father, and with his Son Jesus Christ: and these things we write that our joy may be made full.

And this is the message which we have heard from him, and announce unto you, that God is light, and in him is no darkness at all. If we say that we have fellowship with him and walk in the darkness, we lie, and do not the truth: but if we walk in the light, as he is in the light, we have fellowship one with another, and the blood of Jesus his Son cleanseth us from all sin.—*I John 1: 1–7*

Consider the interpretation of the Christian life suggested here, that it is a life of friendly fellowship with the Father. *Is there not Someone in your heart who warns you against evil, who rebukes you when you sin, who allures you with ideals of what you ought to be, who insists when you are discouraged that you can win yet, and who never entirely gives you up, no matter what you do!* You cannot explain this voice by calling it Conscience; it is Someone who is trying to befriend you. Are you in fellowship with this Invisible Companion? Are you making it easy for him to speak to you; are you giving him quiet hours when he has a chance to be heard; and are you walking with him in service, so that you know the fellowship of which Paul wrote, "We are God's fellow-workers"?

❧❧❧

❖ Seventh Day, Ninth Week

If I speak with the tongues of men and of angels, but have not love, I am become sounding brass, or a clanging cymbal. And if I have the gift of prophecy, and know all mysteries and all knowledge; and if I have all faith, so as to remove mountains, but have not love, I am nothing. And if I bestow all my goods to feed the poor, and if I give my body to be burned, but have not love, it profiteth me nothing. Love suffereth long, and is kind; love envieth not; love vaunteth not itself, is not puffed up, doth not behave itself unseemly, seeketh not its own, is not provoked, taketh not account of evil; rejoiceth not in unrighteousness, but rejoiceth with the truth; beareth all things, believeth all things, hopeth all things, endureth all things. Love never faileth: but whether there be prophecies, they shall be done away; whether there be tongues, they shall cease; whether there be knowledge, it shall be done away. For we know in part, and we prophesy in part; but when that which is perfect is come, that which is in part shall be done away. When I was a child, I spake as a child, I felt as a child, I thought as a child: now that I am become a man, I have put away childish things. For now we see in a mirror, darkly; but then face to face: now I know in part; but then shall I know fully even as also I was fully known. But now abideth faith, hope, love, these three; and the greatest of these is love.—*I Cor. 13*

Some one has said that the Master sat for the portrait which Paul has painted here. Whether Paul consciously was thinking of his words as descriptive of Jesus or not, they certainly are a true portrayal of our Lord's spirit. Read over the description of love's expression in life, beginning, "Love suffereth long and is kind," and think carefully of the way the different phrases of the description fit the Master's character as you know it. Some of the virtues here enumerated are more often praised than practised, and we may well search our own lives by comparing them with the length and breadth and depth and height of the love revealed in Jesus.

❧❧❧

Comment for the Week

The stern qualities of the Master, such as his fearlessness, have often been lost sight of in the emphasis placed upon the tenderer aspects of his character. The pathetic appeal of the suffering Savior, "Is it nothing to you, all ye that pass by?" has been stressed in ecclesiastical ritual and art, and even radical critics have allowed their impressions of Jesus to be dominated by the charm of his gentleness, his meekness and love. So Renan says, as we have quoted, that "Tenderness of heart was in him transformed into infinite sweetness, vague poetry, universal charm"; and Strauss remarks, "Jesus appears as a naturally lovely character which needed but to unfold and to become conscious of itself."[1] Against this too saccharine interpretation of the Master's spirit we have done well to guard ourselves by considering such austere qualities in him as his indignation, his loyalty, his self-restraint, his fearlessness; but this exclusive stress would spoil our picture of our Lord, if we did not consider his overflowing tenderness, his warmly affectionate nature, that quality of which Tennyson says:

> Gentleness,
> Which, when it weds with manhood, makes the man.

The study of this quality in the Master leads us at once away from the extensive, worldwide aspects of his mission to those intimate personal relationships in which he revealed the peculiar beauty of his friendliness. Theology has naturally emphasized his unbounded love, which took the whole race for its object, and in which God revealed his care for the world. When, however, we step into the gospels, we find him dealing in unusual tenderness with individual children; disregarding even excessive weariness and hunger to give gracious service to an unworthy woman (John 4: 6ff); enjoying the hospitable friendship of a favorite family (John 11: 5); and saying to his disciples in words whose depth of affection can hardly be exaggerated, "No longer do I call you servants;... but I have called you friends" (John 15: 15). Everywhere he leaves the impression of affectionate good-will, not scattered and diffuse, comprehending all men in a vague generosity of sentiment, but concrete and particular, seeking special men and women for its objects. In a cross section of his prayer, when alone upon the hillside he communed with God, one would surely have found individual names—some blind Bartimaeus, some child he had met yesterday, and especially the inner circle of his friends. If the field was the world, as he said, the Master's immediate personal relationships were the gardens where the plants of kindness and goodwill were prepared for

1. Francis A. Peabody, *Jesus Christ and the Christian Character*, p. 47.

transplanting to the larger soil. The words of Alice Freeman Palmer are a true expression of his feeling and his method: "It is people that count, you want to put yourself into people; they touch other people; these others still, and so you go on working forever."[2]

He always seems to have felt a special sympathy with widows, facing the problem which Mary faced in bringing up her family.

The affectionate nature of the Master is revealed in his relationships with his home. After the family's visit to Jerusalem when Jesus was twelve years old, we hear no more of Joseph. He never appears again in the gospel record, and the inference is fair that he died in the early youth of the Master. Indeed the suggestion is plausible that Jesus' reason for delaying his public ministry until he was thirty years of age is to be sought in the fact, that on him, as the eldest son and head of the household, devolved the burden of the family's support until the other brothers had grown to manhood. Amid the humble surroundings of an artisan's house in Nazareth, with a large family of brothers and sisters and a widowed mother (Matt. 13: 55, 56), Jesus did the work of a carpenter to maintain the home. The marks of his handicraft and of his early days of life among poor, plain people are evident in his metaphors and parables. He notes the kind of foundations on which a house is built (Matt. 7: 24ff); he understands the necessity of figuring carefully on cost before undertaking to build (Luke 14: 28). He is acquainted with foxes and their lairs, birds and their nests (Matt. 8: 20), hens and their solicitude over their brood (Matt. 23: 37), and the agriculture of a peasant farmer is his familiar field of illustration. He knows well the cost of sparrows, sold as cheap food, in the market place (Matt. 10: 29), and in the home he has seen his mother mend garments until they were past mending, and no new patches could be put on them (Matt. 9: 16). He always seems to have felt a special sympathy with widows, facing the problem which Mary faced in bringing up her family. This sympathy, perhaps is reflected in his feeling toward the widow who cast her mites into the temple treasury, giving a gift worth more in his sight than all the offerings of the millionaires (Mark 12: 42), and in his indignation at those who cover with pious practices the robbery of widows' houses (Mark 12: 40). When the Master wants to picture helplessness crying persistently for relief, he pictures a widow importunately besieging a judge with her petitions (Luke 18: 1ff), and it may be that this was a recollection of some actual incident in the life of his widowed mother.

---

2. Editor: Alice Freeman Palmer (1855-1902) pioneered university education for women. At 26 she became president of Wellesley College and in 1892 she became Dean of Women at the University of Chicago.

The   Manhood   of   the   Master

When one considers the tenderness of Jesus toward little children he can hardly fail to feel that this quality began its expression back in the Nazareth home where the Master was practically the father of the family. The eighteenth chapter of Matthew lets us deeply into the unusual affection of Jesus for children. A child's humility, teachableness and artless sincerity are to him the best symbols of the quality which is necessary for entrance into the Kingdom (v. 2–5). To wrong a child seems to him a crime so heinous that no punishment can be too severe for the man who has deliberately done it, and no self-sacrifice can be too great, even cutting off a hand or plucking out an eye, if necessary to prevent harm to "these little ones" (v. 6–10). Every child is so valuable that to save him a man might well seek for him, as a shepherd, leaving ninety-nine safe sheep, would look for one lost lamb (v. 12, 13). And the Father's special love singles out each one of the children and desires his safety (v. 14). In Mark, this affection of the Master toward the children is put into a picture, the like of which in Plato or Aristotle is to any one who knows ancient thought about childhood unimaginable: "He took them in his arms, and blessed them, laying his hands upon them" (Mark 10: 16). Such a feeling for children as this must have grown in the home life at Nazareth.

To wrong a child seems to him a crime so heinous that no punishment can be too severe for the man who has deliberately done it, and no self-sacrifice can be too great, even cutting off a hand or plucking out an eye, if necessary to prevent harm to "these little ones."

There are passages in the gospels which at first sight seem to negative [negate] such a representation of the feeling of Jesus for his home. *How can this tenderness toward his family have been characteristic of one who said: "If any man cometh unto me, and hateth not his own father, and mother, and wife, and children, and brethren, and sisters, yea, and his own life also, he cannot be my disciple"?* (Luke 14: 26). Again and again Jesus made willingness to leave one's family the test of discipleship, until often in Christendom the monastery has seemed to many nobler than a normal home life, and the founding of a family has been regarded as a concession to physical necessity. Such an interpretation of the Master, however, is plainly untrue. Note that in the text just quoted a man is to hate his family in exactly the same sense in which he is to hate "his own life." That is, the Master is here demanding devotion to his Cause in terms as absolute and searching as he can find. He is thinking of those things which it costs most to surrender, the supremely dear and precious possessions of humanity. He is saying that not even the most beautiful relationships may stand between a man and his loyalty to the Kingdom when the two conflict. And when he thus thinks of what it was hardest for him to surrender, what it is hardest for any right-minded man to give up, he selects as the most precious things in human experience the ties of the family and one's own life. *This text is an exaltation of the home, not a depreciation of it.* Jesus is here purposely putting self-sacrifice in its most difficult form by asking men to be willing to surrender what is most valuable on earth, short of the Kingdom, a happy family life. Jesus felt what Mazzini felt when he wrote: *"He who through fatality of circumstances cannot live the serene life of family, has a void in his heart, that nothing fills; and I who write these pages, well I know it!"*

When in the light of this interpretation we look at the Master's life of public ministry, many of his words and actions gain a fresh and significant meaning. When he said, "The foxes have holes, and the birds of the heaven have nests; but the Son of man hath not where to lay his head," he was lonesome for a home. When at Bethany he welcomed the family of Lazarus and his sisters as a haven of retreat, he was indulging a love of home life from which he had been shut out for years. When he bitterly assailed the divorce customs of his people and pleaded for the ideal of an indissoluble bond between man and wife, he was speaking from his heart's love for a true home (Mark 10: 5–9). When he vehemently rebuked the Pharisees for their tradition, according to which a man, if he said Corban, need make no provision for his parents (Mark 7: 10–12); when he included "Honor thy father and thy mother" among the commandments needful to eternal life (Matt. 19: 19); when with grief he foresaw that one effect of his revolutionary gospel would be to break up families (Luke 12: 53); when he expressed his overflowing gratitude to those who for his sake had left "house, or brethren, or sisters, or mother, or father, or children, or lands" (Mark 10: 29, 30); he was revealing his profound love of a home. Above all, when his home folk came to call him away from his mission and he could not avoid a clash, it must have been one of the deepest sacrifices of his life (Mark 3: 21, 31–35).

It is people that count, you want to put yourself into people; they touch other people; these others still, and so you go on working forever.—Alice Freeman Palmer

---

From then on, he defined utter devotion in terms of being willing to give up one's family. What abiding tenderness he felt toward the old ties is revealed when upon the cross, amid his agony, he made provision for his mother in the home of John (John 19: 26, 27).

Indeed, the Master's most characteristic teaching is couched in family terms, his methods are the methods of the home, and his ideal for all humanity is a family ideal. His dominant thought of God is neither as a King nor as a judge, but as a Father. His controlling thought of man is always couched in terms of brotherhood, and to the correct and exclusive elder son, who said when the prodigal returned, "This thy son," Jesus made the, father say, "This thy brother" (Luke 15: 29ff). Fatherhood and brotherhood comprehended his thought of God and man. Moreover many of the Master's most characteristic ideas and methods are peculiar to the family life. In a true home every person is of infinite value, and the safety of all the other children cannot satisfy the parents' hearts if one is lost. This spirit the Master applied to all humanity (Luke 15: 3–10). In a true home personal influence is the transforming power, and this Jesus adopted as his method, whether with his disciples when he "appointed twelve, that they might be with him" (Mark 3: 14), or in his plan for their future work, when he said, "Ye are the light of the world," and "Ye are the salt of the earth." Only in a home are relationships indissoluble so that a bad son is still a son, and an evil brother still a brother. David is expressing the peculiar quality of family relationship, as distinguished from the tie of master and servant, King and subject, judge and culprit, when over his treacherous and rebellious boy he cries, "O Absalom, my son, my son!" This attitude Jesus carries out to all mankind and teaches alike God's exhaustless grace for man and man's illimitable service and forgiveness of his brethren. And when we seek in a single phrase to summarize Jesus' ideal for humanity, there is none better than to call it the "familyizing" of the world,—one Father, all men brothers, and every relationship tuned to the spiritual meaning of that family bond. Out of what tenderness of heart, as well as greatness of faith and hope, did these terms and methods and ideals of the Master spring.

Only in a home are relationships indissoluble so that a bad son is still a son, and an evil brother still a brother.

The affection of Jesus is revealed also in the strength and quality of his friendships. The extensiveness, the lavish breadth and generosity, of Jesus' love for all men is perhaps the most familiar element in his character, and the Christian Church has always emphasized the title which now she has put into a hymn,

O, Thou great Friend to all the sons of men.

But in a more intimate way the quality of the Master's tenderness is shown in his special love for those few men to whom he was drawn by the gravitation of spiritual sympathy. Of all his followers, twelve stood closest to him, and of these twelve three belonged to the inner circle of his friends. Peter, James and John were deepest in his fellowship; for all the imperfection of their insight they understood him best; and when he entered some great experience of spiritual exaltation, as on the Mount of Transfiguration (Mark 9: 2ff), or did an act of mercy in the intimacy of a family circle, where only closest friends have a right to come (Mark 5: 37), or faced the supreme struggle of his life in Gethsemane (Mark 14: 32, 33), these three were specially selected to be with him.

What he meant to his friends, the consequences of his influence on them make plain. He believed in them and their hidden possibilities when they did not even believe in themselves (Luke 5: 8–10); he kept them in his fellowship that they might catch the spirit of his life (Mark 3: 14), and he trained them for service, alike by setting them at work (Mark 6: 7ff), and by calling them apart for quiet retreats of conference and prayer (Mark 6: 31); he prayed for them when he was alone (Luke 22: 32), and when he gathered with them for the last time he offered a prayer for them in their hearing, the spirit of which is inexpressibly tender and solicitous (John 17). All the qualities that make deep friendship beautiful are present in the Master's love for his disciples; fidelity that will not give up even Judas until a last word of affection fails to shame him from his treacherous deed (Matt. 26: 50); unflattering honesty that rebukes the evil of a friend's life when it would have been easier to condone (Mark 8: 33); deathless solicitude that desires to watch over and protect them, "even unto the end of the world" (Matt. 28: 20); and sacrificial devotion which not only speaks but fulfils in deed that greatest love, "that a man lay down his life for his friends" (John 15: 13).

All this meaning that the Master's friendship had for his disciples is often emphasized, but not so often the meaning that their friendship had for him. It was the one earthly comfort of his life, after his public ministry began. He looked round on his disciples and called them his mother and his sisters and his brethren (Matt. 12: 49, 50); he was not content until they were more than servants and disciples, he wanted them for friends (John 15: 14, 15); he found his great encouragement when they showed some deepening insight into his meaning (Matt. 16: 15–17) or when the work which he entrusted to them was well done (Luke 10: 17–20); he was grateful beyond measure for their loyalty (Mark 10: 29, 30), and with peculiar tenderness spoke of them as "they that have continued with me in my temptations" (Luke 22: 28). He relied on them to carry on his work when he was gone, and with all his deep dependence upon God, he turned gratefully to them for human sympathy and understanding. When the last night came, his heart overflowed with unspeakable longing, as he said to them, "With desire I have desired to eat this passover with you before I suffer" (Luke 22: 15). On that night when everything else was being taken from him he counted his wealth in his friendships; "Thine they were," he said in thanks to his Father, "and thou gavest them to me" (John 17: 6). The whole impression of Jesus' intimate relationship with his disciples is one of deepest personal affection, the sort of warm, compelling friendliness that calls out in answer an undying loyalty. That the disciple whom Jesus loved best should have leaned upon his breast at supper (John 13: 23–35), is but symbolical of this wonderful relationship.

On that night when everything else was being taken from him he counted his wealth in his friendships; "Thine they were," he said in thanks to his Father, "and thou gavest them to me."

No relationship ever is complete until it has grown into friendliness. There have been many brothers and sisters in the world, but when we think of that natural kinship at its best, we remember special names, Felix Mendelssohn and his sister Fanny, Charles Lamb and his sister Mary, William Wordsworth and his sister Dorothy; or, perhaps, Catherine Boyle and her brother Robert, of whom Bishop Burnett said, "Such a sister became such a brother and it was suitable to both their characters that they should have improved the relationship under which they were born to the more exalted and endearing one of friend."[3] There have been many wives and husbands in the world, but only in marriages like those of Charles Kingsley and Fanny Grenfell, Robert Browning and Elizabeth Barrett, William Gladstone and Catherine Glynn, where the relationship of marriage was the cusp in which the flower of friendship grew, do we feel the meaning of wedded love truly consummated. So a father may be to his children simply the progenitor, or the provider, or the disciplinarian, but the natural bond of parenthood is never fulfilled until it has been exalted into friendship. Even the relationship between a sovereign and subject finds its nobler meaning when Tennyson can write as he did to Queen Victoria: "I will not say that I am loyal or that your Majesty is gracious, for those are terms used or abused by every courtier, but I will say that during our conversation I felt the touch of that true friendship that binds human hearts together whether they be Kings or cobblers." So the sacred relationship of Lord and Master which Jesus bore to his disciples was in itself inadequate. He sought for friends. And ever since, the spiritual seers of Christendom have defined the deepest meanings of the Christian life in terms of friendship with God and with his Son.

Ꝑ∙Ꝑ∙Ꝑ

---

3. Henry Clay Trumbull, *Friendship, the Master Passion,* p. 111.

WEEK

10

The Master's Scale of Values

What did the priest and Levite do that stirred the Master's disapproval? They did nothing. That was the sole fault with them. They endeavored to be neutral when a concrete example was presented to them of the warfare of evil on men; they simply went by on the other side.

Daily Readings

❖ First Day, Tenth Week

Lay not up for yourselves treasures upon the earth, where moth and rust consume, and where thieves break through and steal: but lay up for yourselves treasures in heaven, where neither moth nor rust doth consume, and where thieves do not break through nor steal: for where thy treasure is, there will thy heart be also. The lamp of the body is the eye: if therefore thine eye be single, thy whole body shall be full of light. But if thine eye be evil, thy whole body shall be full of darkness. If therefore the light that is in thee be darkness, how great is the darkness! No man can serve two masters: for either he will hate the one, and love the other; or else he will hold to one, and despise the other. Ye cannot serve God and mammon.—*Matt. 6: 19–24*

How often we desire two mutually exclusive things: evil pleasures and a clear conscience, self-indulgence and good health, laziness and success, a selfish, worldly life and a consciousness of serving God! *Men everywhere are trying to possess themselves of two things that exclude each other and they always fail. They have to take one or the other. The central lesson of life is that we must choose.* If I want to be both an easy-going drifter and a successful physician, I must choose between them, and let my desire for one be utterly subordinated to my devotion for the other. Between a covetous, self-indulging, superficial worldliness and a devout, unselfish service of God and his Cause in the earth, there can be no satisfactory compromise. We cannot do both. Our heart's real treasure will be in one place or the other. We must choose.

৵৵৵

❖ Second Day, Tenth Week

Therefore I say unto you, Be not anxious for your life, what ye shall eat, or what ye shall drink; nor yet for your body, what ye shall put on. Is not the life more than the food, and the body than the raiment? Behold the birds of the heaven, that they sow not, neither do they reap, nor gather into barns; and your heavenly Father feedeth them. Are not ye of much more value than they? And which of you by being anxious can add one cubit unto the measure of his life? And why are ye anxious concerning raiment? Consider the lilies of the field, how they grow; they toil not, neither do they spin: yet I say unto you, that even Solomon in all his glory was not arrayed like one of these. But if God doth so clothe the grass of the field, which to-day is, and tomorrow is cast into the oven, shall he not much more clothe you, O ye of little faith? Be not therefore anxious, saying, What shall we eat? or, What shall we drink? or, Wherewithal shall we be clothed? For after all these things do the Gentiles seek; for your heavenly Father knoweth that ye have need of all these things. But seek ye first his kingdom, and his righteousness; and all these things shall be added unto you.—*Matt. 6: 25–33*

The truth of yesterday may be restated today in terms of the last verse of our Scripture. Only one thing can be first in any man's scale of values. *There must, to be sure, be many different ranges and grades of interest in any human life, physical welfare, recreation, pleasure—"your heavenly Father knoweth that ye have need of all these things"—but only one thing can be first. The Cause of God on the earth should be first, says Jesus, and all other things subordinated in due proportion to it.* Nothing good is by this necessarily excluded from life. Rather in ordinary experience, health, comfort, recreation, money, family love are all glorified by being made ministers to the Cause of God on earth and the Cause of God on earth aims among other things at health, comfort, and a fine family life for all. But even when it costs, the Kingdom alone must be put first in our lives and for the sake of it all evil things excluded and all good things subordinated. Consider what this means particularly to you. Try to express in simple language exactly what is involved in putting the Kingdom of God first in all of the varied experiences of daily life.

৵৵৵

❖ Third Day, Tenth Week

But he said unto him, A certain man made a great supper; and he bade many: and he sent forth his servant at supper time to say to them that were bidden, Come; for all things are now ready. And they all with one consent began to make excuse. The first said unto him, I have bought a field, and I must needs go out and see it; I pray thee have me excused. And another said, I have bought five yoke of oxen, and I go to prove them; I pray thee have me excused. And another said, I have married a wife, and therefore I cannot come. And the servant came, and told his lord these things. Then the master of the house being angry said to his servant, Go out quickly into the streets and lanes of the city, and bring in hither the poor and maimed and blind and lame. And the servant said, Lord, what thou didst command is done, and yet there is room. And the lord said unto the servant, Go out into the highways and hedges, and constrain them to come in, that my house may be filled. For I say unto you, that none of those men that were bidden shall taste of my supper.—*Luke 14: 16–24*

Were any of the men who refused the invitation doing wrong things? On the contrary their business and family zeal was commendable. Only they were so completely preoccupying their lives with lesser things that the more important things were crowded out.

To dress, to call, to dine, to break
    No canon of the social code,
The little laws that lacqueys make,
    The futile decalogue of Mode,—
How many a soul for these things lives
    With pious passion, grave intent!

        * * * * *

And never ev'n in dreams has seen
    The things that are more excellent

Consider that our life time and life energy are limited, that if we preoccupy them with little things, the great things will be lost, that as Ruskin says about reading, "Do you not know that if you read this book, you cannot read that?" Are you emphasizing the things that are more excellent?

༜༜༜

❖ Fourth Day, Tenth Week

When any one heareth the word of the kingdom, and understandeth it not, then cometh the evil one, and snatcheth away that which hath been sown in his heart. This is he that was sown by the way side. And he that was sown upon the rocky places, this is he that heareth the word, and straightway with joy receiveth it; yet hath he not root in himself, but endureth for awhile; and when tribulation or persecution ariseth because of the word, straightway he stumbleth. And he that was sown among the thorns, this is he that heareth the word; and the care of the world, and the deceitfulness of riches, choke the word, and he becometh unfruitful. And he that was sown upon the good ground, this is he that heareth the word, and understandeth it; who verily beareth fruit, and bringeth forth, some a hundredfold, some sixty, some thirty.—*Matt. 13: 19–23*

Think especially of the seed that fell among thorns, and let it illustrate afresh the thought of yesterday. The seed found the ground preoccupied and so was crowded out. Are not many of our most tragic failures caused by excessive busyness, not necessarily with unworthy things, but with less worthy things, until our prayer life, our trust in God, our finest spiritual quality, our unselfishness are choked and die? Schiller says that you can tell an artist by what he leaves out. He does not crowd everything into his picture helter-skelter; he chooses a central and dominant feature and subordinates everything else to it. *Are you living your life with a true sense of proportion? You have not time nor strength for everything. Are you putting first things first? Apply this particularly to love of money, love of social eminence, and love of pleasure as competitors against character for the throne of your life.*

❧❧❧

❖ Fifth Day, Tenth Week

And he spake a parable unto them, saying, The ground of a certain rich man brought forth plentifully: and he reasoned within himself, saying, What shall I do, because I have not where to bestow my fruits? And he said, This will I do: I will pull down my barns, and build greater; and there will I bestow all my grain and my goods. And I will say to my soul, Soul, thou hast much goods laid up for many years; take thine ease, eat, drink, be merry. But God said unto him, Thou foolish one, this night is thy soul required of thee; and the things which thou hast prepared, whose shall they be? So is he that layeth up treasure for himself, and is not rich toward God.—*Luke 12: 16–21*

As we turn to consider the things which the Master put first, we find that in the individual life a useful, pure and worthy character was to him clearly supreme. Wealth in lands and crops and pleasures did not compare with it. Indeed in this passage a man not inwardly rich toward God in character, who trusts in money as his treasure, is called foolish. Think of the ways in which you are tempted to make money your goal in life. Is there any way of conquering this temptation save by positively devoting yourself to the Christian Cause, and making money the servant of your spiritual devotion? *Put money in servile livery and it will do great work; but let it usurp the crown and a man is spiritually doomed.*

❧❧❧

❖ Sixth Day, Tenth Week

The thief cometh not, but that he may steal, and kill, and destroy: I came that they may have life, and may have it abundantly. I am the good shepherd: the good shepherd layeth down his life for the sheep. He that is a hireling, and not a shepherd, whose own the sheep are not, beholdeth the wolf coming, and leaveth the sheep, and fleeth, and the wolf snatcheth them, and scattereth them: he fleeth because he is a hireling, and careth not for the sheep. I am the good shepherd; and I know mine own, and mine own know me, even as the Father knoweth me, and I know the Father; and I lay down my life for the sheep. And other sheep I have, which are not of this fold: them also I must bring, and they shall hear my voice; and they shall become one flock, one shepherd.—*John 10: 10–16*

See in this passage a revelation of the Master's scale of values. The lives of people were to him of ineffable worth; therefore no sacrifice was too great to save them. You can feel at once the transcendent importance of having a true idea of what is worth most, for we always sacrifice our secondary values to our primary ones. *Jesus was willing to make any sacrifice to save people. Money, comfort, pleasure, his own earthly existence, anything he would surrender if the sacrifice would help to save people.* He felt the spiritual life of men to be holy ground; he felt all sin there to be sacrilege; he felt all injustice done to men to be the violation of a sacred place, and he counted any price worth while that protected and redeemed the lives of men. *Can you see any signs in your life that you share very vitally the Master's idea of this supremely valuable thing?*

❧❧❧

❖ Seventh Day, Tenth Week

Jesus made answer and said, A certain man was going down from Jerusalem to Jericho; and he fell among robbers, who both stripped him and beat him, and departed, leaving him half dead. And by chance a certain priest was going down that way: and when he saw him, he passed by on the other side. And in like manner a Levite also, when he came to the place, and saw him, passed by on the other side. But a certain Samaritan, as he journeyed, came where he was: and when he saw him, he was moved with compassion, and came to him, and bound up his wounds, pouring on them oil and wine; and he set him on his own beast, and brought him to an inn, and took care of him. And on the morrow he took out two shillings, and gave them to the host, and said, Take care of him; and whatsoever thou spendest more, I, when I come back again, will repay thee. Which of these three, thinkest thou, proved neighbor unto him that fell among the robbers? And he said, He that showed mercy on him. And Jesus said unto him, Go, and do thou likewise.—*Luke 10: 30–37*

What did the priest and Levite do that stirred the Master's disapproval? *They did nothing.* That was the sole fault with them. They endeavored to be neutral when a concrete example was presented to them of the warfare of evil on men; they simply went by on the other side. Does not attempted neutrality always fail so? The priest and Levite have been rightly coupled ever since with the robbers, as supporters of wrong in the world. No man can really be neutral. As Jesus says in the next chapter: "He that is not with me is against me; and he that gathereth not with me scattereth" (Luke 11: 23). *A great war is on between good and evil, between Christ and anti-Christ. The battlefield is in you and around you. Your thoughts and deeds inevitably ore taking sides. Have you settled the matter once for all as to which side you will be on, with all your strength? Have you deliberately put God and his Cause first!*

శ్రీశ్రీశ్రీ

Comment for the Week

It is the commonplace of our teaching that belief in the Lord Jesus is the means of entrance into the Christian life. We should note, however, that in our day it is very possible for a man to profess belief in our Lord without sharing deeply the searching experience of the men who followed him in Palestine. Men may believe in him today in an appreciative way as the very best character that ever lived; they may stand before his life as they might before a beautiful picture or poem, saying, "It is very well done!" Or men may believe in him as represented in some creedal formula, such as "Very God of very God, begotten not made; "they may recite with intellectual assent the borrowed results of others' attempts to comprehend Christ's theological significance. But both these sets of men may utterly miss the central effect of Jesus on his first followers; that he demanded a revolution in their standards of value, that he took things commonly put first and subordinated them, while things long neglected he counted of preeminent worth. He found men anxiously consuming all their energies in accumulating the externals of life, food and clothing, and he tried to recentralize their lives around a more valuable object of devotion: "Seek ye first his kingdom" (Matt. 6: 33). He found men regarding the keeping of a Sabbath law as more important than the helping of a man, and he insisted on turning right side up this perverted scale of values: "The sabbath was made for man, and not man for the sabbath" (Mark 2: 27). *Everywhere we find him elevating certain values as worthy of absolute devotion, and subordinating others as secondary; everywhere we find his standards of what is important and what is unimportant so new and revolutionary that the acceptance of them meant a complete transformation in the lives of men.* Long before Peter started the Christian creed by affirming that Jesus was the Christ (Mark 8: 29), Peter had felt this primary demand of Jesus that men must change their ideas of what is really valuable in life.

Moreover, we discover that this effect of the Master on his followers was deliberate. When he said, "Where thy treasure is, there will thy heart be also" (Matt. 6: 21), he distinctly recognized that a man's scale of values is the determining factor in his life. *Behind all professed beliefs lies this deeper matter: What is it that a man counts so worth while that he is subordinating other things to it?* Now, when the Master thus set himself to change the location of men's "treasure," to reconstruct the standards of value by which men were living, he furnished us with one of the best means of understanding his own character. What better way is there of estimating the quality of any man, than by discovering the things that he counts most worth while? We may apply the Master's own principle to himself: when we know where his treasure is, we shall find where his heart is also.

He died for men because he believed that men were worth dying for.

In one significant statement Jesus has told us clearly his estimation of the supremely valuable treasure: "What shall a man be profited, if he shall gain the whole world, and forfeit his life?" (Matt. 16: 26). It is needless to say that the life to which the Master here refers is not alone the physical but the spiritual, not merely the existence of the body but the character and quality of the self. That to him was of supreme value. Nothing was to be compared with it. To cut off a hand or pluck out an eye was a sacrifice readily to be made if the spiritual quality of the man required it (Matt. 5: 29, 30). This real self, this invisible, spiritual personality made in the image of God, intended for his character, and sure to live forever, was so infinitely valuable, in the thought of the Master, that he tried continually, by every manner of statement, to make his disciples feel with him that everything else in life must be subordinated to the interests of this supreme treasure. He told them that God ranked personality as preeminently valuable: worth more than flowers, "If God doth so clothe the grass of the field, which today is and tomorrow is cast into the oven, shall he not much more clothe you?" (Matt. 6: 30); worth more than sparrows, "Ye are of more value than many sparrows" (Matt. 10: 31) worth more than sheep, "How much then is a man of more value than a sheep!" (Matt. 12: 12); worth more than the most sacred religious institution, "The sabbath was made for man, and not man for the sabbath" (Mark 2: 27); worth so much that the transformation of even one life sets all heaven to singing, "I say unto you, that even so there shall be joy in heaven over one sinner that repenteth" (Luke 15: 7–10).

That the supreme value for the Master was personal character is shown in his own life even more than in his teaching. The passion of his life was saviorhood. The church has often stereotyped the title, Savior, and made it cold and official in theological theory; but at first it was not theology, at all. Saviorhood was the vivid and immediate impression of the Master's daily living. The manifest joy of his life was in saving and serving men. "The Son of man also came not to be ministered unto, but to minister, and to give his life a ransom for many" (Mark 10: 45); "The Son of man came to seek and to save that which was lost" (Luke 19: 10); these are no isolated and occasional notes, but rather the continually recurrent theme of his living. He ministered to personality through the body and spent a large portion of his waking hours in healing men's physical ailments (Mark 6: 54–56); he ministered to men's spiritual life directly in all his preaching. Always the supreme value for which he lived and taught and sacrificed was personality, marred and estranged, yet even so the child of God, loved by the Father and possessing everlasting issues of weal and woe. And all this sacrifice was founded on his scale of values. *He died for men because he believed that men were worth dying for.*

In endeavoring to win acceptance for a standard of values in which personal character would thus have an absolute supremacy, the Master faced one preeminent enemy. That enemy he called mammon, which is simply an old Aramaic word for riches. Men had their treasure in the earthly life "where moth and rust consume, and where thieves break through and steal" (Matt. 6: 19). They put money above character, wealth above spiritual life; their controlling scale of value had riches at the top. We cannot understand the Master's attitude toward wealth until we see that he felt "the deceitfulness of riches" (Mark 4: 19) to be the chief enemy that he had to meet in persuading men to count character the most valuable thing in life. He saw men in whom all possibility of fine living was being smothered by unnecessary anxiety for worldly goods (Matt. 6: 31); he saw the royal invitation to a spiritual life refused because men were preoccupied with lesser things and had their perspective of values all awry (Luke 14: 18ff); he saw men forgetting the sacredest privileges of brotherhood in their covetous desire for wealth, men at last reduced to offering to their souls nothing but money, ease, merriment, and corn (Luke

12: 16ff); he became indignant with Pharisees who in pride made wealth a substitute for real and inward goodness (Matt. 6: 2ff), and he was sorrowful when repeatedly he saw fine beginnings in the spiritual life choked, as with thorns, by "the care of the world and the deceitfulness of riches" (Matt. 13: 22). When the writer of I Timothy says that "the love of money is a root of all kinds of evil" (I Tim. 6: 10), he is making the same observation that his Master made. At every point the chief enemy of Jesus' scale of values was the love of money.

But the insistent emphasis of his life was that the "true riches" were not money but character, and that no sacrifice could be too great, if it was necessary to maintain the supremacy of the spirit and to achieve the subordination of all secondary things.

At times the conflict between these two standards seemed so difficult of solution that Jesus despaired of the men who had riches: "Verily I say unto you, It is hard for a rich man to enter into the kingdom of heaven. And again I say unto you, It is easier for a camel to go through a needle's eye, than for a rich man to enter into the kingdom of God" (Matt. 19: 23, 24). This discouraged exclamation was wrung from him when a rich ruler, ready to listen to the Master, to appreciate him, to believe in him, was not yet ready to accept his scale of values and put money in a secondary place. Perhaps it was a similar experience that caused the Master's outburst, reported alone by Luke: "Blessed are ye poor: for yours is the kingdom of God.... But woe unto you that are rich!" (Luke 6: 20–24).

So Jesus hated covetousness as a mother hates the disease that is despoiling her children's lives. When, however, he found men who were the masters, not the slaves of their possessions, he rejoiced and took them as his examples of right living. To the men who looked on money as an entrustment from God, and so used it, he said, "Well done, good and faithful servant!" (Matt. 25: 21–23). He made the right use of money one of the tests of God's confidence in men, and said, "If therefore, ye have not been faithful in the unrighteous mammon, who will commit to your trust the true riches?" (Luke 16: 11). *But the insistent emphasis of his life was that the "true riches" were not money but character, and that no sacrifice could be too great, if it was necessary to maintain the supremacy of the spirit and to achieve the subordination of all secondary things.*

We have been speaking of personality as the supreme value in life for Jesus, but more is involved in this than the individual man; the social life of the race is implied in it. Side by side with personality in his scale of values, the Master put the coming Kingdom of God. *He who said that it was profitless to gain the whole world and lose one's self, said also, "Seek first the kingdom of God, and his righteousness." The first was the Master's supreme evaluation of character in persons, the second, of character in society.* Here, once more, all lesser worths were to be subordinated, even to be sacrificed, for the sake of this most valuable of all social treasures, the reign of righteousness in the relationships of men. "The kingdom of heaven," said Jesus, "is like unto a treasure, hidden in the field; which a man found, and hid; and in his joy he goeth and selleth all that he hath, and buyeth that field" (Matt. 13: 44). Nothing in life is too precious to be surrendered for the Kingdom's sake. This standard of value, so distinctly stated in his teaching, is in Jesus' life everywhere incarnate. His own comfort, his home life, his reputation, the most sacred institutions of his people, everything was subordinated to this central devotion of the Master to the Kingdom. And this consuming loyalty of his was founded on his scale of values. *He died for the Kingdom because he thought that the Kingdom was worth dying for.*

Once more in this endeavor to give a new perspective to man's sense of life's values, the Master found his archenemy in mammon. Everywhere he saw the lust for riches ruthlessly riding over the social life of men, and spoiling the brotherhood of God's children. He saw rich men made so unfraternal by the self-indulgence which their wealth made possible, that they were callous even in the presence of manifest misery at their very gates (Luke 16: 19ff); he saw men who professed to be religious leaders so spoiled by covetousness that they robbed widows' houses and covered their cruelty with prayer (Mark 12: 40); he saw men who ought to have understood and accepted his standard of worth, made so spiritually blind by avarice that, as Luke puts it, being "lovers of money, they scoffed at him" (Luke 16: 14). Covetousness was ruining the spirit of the Kingdom. It made men exploit even the piety of the common people as the money-changers in the temple did. It incarnated itself in robbers who left their victims half dead on the Jericho road (Luke 10: 30ff). *The greed of men for money seemed to Jesus the great obstacle in the way of their accepting his scale of values.*

The dilemma appeared to him sharp and clear: "Ye cannot serve God and mammon" (Matt. 6: 24). We can serve God with mammon, and we serve mammon with God-given powers; but we cannot serve both. However like an ellipse a man may try to draw his life around two foci, he will magnetize one of them with his devotion until the other is drawn into it, and the life that started as an ellipse will end as a circle around one center. This is the secret of Jesus' austere, forbidding language about wealth. Even in the company of his own disciples he saw the fatal lure of mammon ruining a soul, stealing devotion from the Kingdom to itself. "What are ye willing to give me," said Judas to the priests, "and I will deliver him unto you? And they weighed unto him thirty pieces of silver"

(Matt. 26: 15). Behind the attitude of the Master toward wealth was a deep observation of life and a bitter personal experience. Not as an economist or as the protagonist of a social theory, but as a soul who put righteousness in persons and in society first, did he exclaim, as Mark reports him, "Children, how hard is it for them that trust in riches to enter into the kingdom of God!" (Mark 10: 24).

The feeling of Jesus about avarice is one measure of his positive estimate of personal character and social righteousness as the supremely valuable goods of life. *We must turn, however, to his own abounding sense of living the life most worth while, to see how richly he possessed, not as a matter of theory but of experience, the consciousness of being wealthy himself.* In John's gospel, especially, in such recurring phrases as "I am the life," "I am the bread of life," "I came that they may have life, and may have it abundantly" (John 14: 6; 6: 48; 10: 10), one feels not the word of a soul impoverished by sacrifice, but of a soul conscious of a wealth surpassing all other riches in the world. And back of this Johannine interpretation of the Master, is the same strain running through the earlier biographies. The Master looked on men endeavoring to gain wealth by acquisition of externals, and startled them with his paradox: "Whosoever would save his life shall lose it; and whosoever shall lose his life for my sake and the gospel's shall save it" (Mark 8: 35). To Jesus the life that lost itself in other lives and in devotion to the Kingdom had discovered the secret of great living. Personal character and social righteousness were to him the realest real-estate on earth, the only wealth that lasts forever, and the man who had staked out large claims in this abiding realm was the true millionaire, in this sense the Master felt himself to be very rich. He had indestructible treasures in the heavenly life, he had the "true riches" entrusted to him; he was "rich toward God" (Luke 12: 21). He knew from experience that "a man's life consisteth not in the abundance of the things which he possesseth" (Luke 12: 15), but in that resource of character, that satisfaction in ministry, that cooperation with the Eternal Purpose, that boundless hope, which caused the Scripture's exclamations, "The life which is life indeed!" (I Tim. 6: 19); "He that hath the Son hath the life!" (I John 5: 12).

We must note that the Master did not minimize the physical necessities of man's existence. "Your heavenly Father knoweth that ye have need of these things" (Matt. 6: 32), he said. "When ye pray, say, Give us this day our daily bread." He himself labored with sacrificial fidelity to relieve physical distress, and one has but to walk through the pages of the gospels to find himself in a motley company of the indigent that throng about Jesus. Lepers, destitute through sickness (Luke 5: 12), women incurably ill, all their money spent on the physicians (Luke 8: 43), laborers, idle in the market place, because no one has hired them (Matt. 20: 7), the naked, hungry, thirsty, friendless and imprisoned (Matt. 25: 36ff), the victims of vice who have sold their bodies to satisfy their hunger or their vanity (Matt. 21: 31), the victims of debt, in jail and not to be released until the last farthing is paid (Matt. 5: 25, 26), all these are in the gospels, drawn there by the gravitation of the Master's care and sympathy. He knew the crushing burden of economic need; he never belittled the awfulness of poverty; you have but to read his parable of the talents or his story of the man shrewd enough to invest money in making friends (Luke 16: 9), to see that he regarded what we commonly call "goods" as really good. But freedom from economic need was not "true riches" in the Master's thought. Only the investment of life in personal character and social righteousness could bring real wealth. That was treasure "where neither moth nor rust doth consume, and where thieves do not break through nor steal," and when the lesser goods conflicted with the supreme values the Master "with joy sold all that he had" to possess himself of the things most worth while.

Who can stand before the Master's scale of values and be unashamed? Even through commonest daily life the choices run, which, if we say we are his disciples, must be brought to the arbitrament of his standards of worth. *"First things first!"* is his demand, and no formal ritual or intellectual assent to creedal statement can blind his eyes to our unchristian scales of value. What is it that we count worth so much that other things are subordinated to it?

> Daughters of Time, the hypocritic Days,
> Muffled and dumb like barefoot dervishes,
> And marching single in an endless file,
> Bring diadems and fagots in their hands.
> To each they offer gifts after his will,
> Bread, kingdoms, stars, and sky that holds them all.
> I, in my pleached garden, watched the pomp,
> Forgot my morning wishes, hastily
> Took a few herbs and apples, and the
> Day Turned and departed silent. I, too late,
> Under her solemn fillet saw the scorn.

૭ન૭ન૭ન

WEEK

11

The Master's Spirit

The Master's preeminence comes not chiefly from his describable virtues, but from those deep sources of his life with God, out of which his virtues flowed, begotten not made, and fragrant, every one of them, with the quality of his perfect fellowship with the Father.

Daily Readings

❖ **First Day, Eleventh Week**

At that season Jesus answered and said, I thank thee, O Father, Lord of heaven and earth, that thou didst hide these things from the wise and understanding, and didst reveal them unto babes: yea, Father, for so it was well-pleasing in thy sight. All things have been delivered unto me of my Father: and no one knoweth the Son, save the Father; neither doth any know the Father, save the Son, and he to whomsoever the Son willeth to reveal him. Come unto me, all ye that labor and are heavy laden, and I will give you rest. Take my yoke upon you, and learn of me; for I am meek and lowly in heart: and ye shall find rest unto your souls. For my yoke is easy, and my burden is light.—*Matt. 11: 25–30*

Is not this a strange combination of ideas? In one breath the Master claims a unique communion with God and in the next he calls himself "meek and lowly in heart." If at first there seems to be a conflict between such a claim and such a profession, consider what humility is. *Is it not at its deepest a quality of spirit that comes from recognizing God as the source of all that is worthy in us, so that we take no credit to ourselves and see no reason for pride, no matter what we may achieve?*

And every virtue we possess,
  And every victory won,
And every thought of holiness
  Are His alone.

This is the spirit of humility. Therefore the more intimate any soul's sense of communion with God, the more meekness and lowliness of heart will result. The real test of humility comes when a man is making a great success and is tempted to forget that all his power is simply an entrustment from God.

ત્રજ્ત્રજ્ત્રજ્

❖ Second Day, Eleventh Week

And he spake a parable unto those that were bidden, when he marked how they chose out the chief seats; saying unto them, When thou art bidden of any man to a marriage feast, sit not down in the chief seat; lest haply a more honorable man than thou be bidden of him., and he that bade thee and him shall come and say to thee, Give this man place; and then thou shalt begin with shame to take the lowest place. But when thou art bidden, go and sit down in the lowest place; that when he that hath bidden thee cometh, he may say to thee, Friend, go up higher: then shalt thou have glory in the presence of all that sit at meat with thee. For every one that exalteth himself shall be humbled; and he that humbleth himself shall be exalted.—*Luke 14: 7–11*

How instinctively we approve the spirit of a humble man! We think all the more of Mr. Gladstone when he accepts a weighty responsibility, saying: "The longer I live the more I feel my utter powerlessness in the House of Commons. But my principle is this: never to shrink from any such responsibility when laid upon me by a competent person." We like Lord Tennyson the better when we learn that he wrote "The Brook," and then threw it in the waste basket because he thought it was not good enough to publish. *We feel instinctively that the best work will be done by men who are humble, that is, who are teachable and aspiring, who compare themselves with the loftiest ideals and know they have not attained their highest, and who feel that the power by which they do their best work is given to them, not created by them. It is to such that even the world says, "Come up higher."*

ત્રજ્ત્રજ્ત્રજ્

❖ Third Day, Eleventh Week

And he said, So is the kingdom of God, as if a man should cast seed upon the earth; and should sleep and rise night and day, and the seed should spring up and grow, he knoweth not how. The earth beareth fruit of herself; first the blade, then the ear, then the full grain in the ear. But when the fruit is ripe, straightway he putteth forth the sickle, because the harvest is come.

And he said, How shall we liken the kingdom of God? or in what parable shall we set it forth? It is like a grain of mustard seed, which, when it is sown upon the earth, though it be less than all the seeds that are upon the earth, yet when it is sown, groweth up, and becometh greater than all the herbs, and putteth out great branches; so that the birds of the heaven can lodge under the shadow thereof.—*Mark 4: 26–32*

No man can make a harvest grow; the vital power is God's, not man's, and man by all his labor simply succeeds in giving God's power a chance. *Consider the universal truth that all man's power is appropriated by him, not created by him.* The difference between a dug-out canoe and an ocean liner is the difference in man's capacity for appropriating universal forces. The difference between a successful tree and a failure lies in vital ability to assimilate nature's power in soil and sunshine. All the best in us is God in us, and our endeavor must always be to appropriate his power. *The great souls always have had this sense of dependence on God. Consider Jesus: "I can of myself do nothing."* Consider Paul: "I live, yet not I, but Christ liveth in me." How inevitably this consciousness makes a noble and worthy humility. Humility is not simply saying, "Sinners, of whom I am chief; "humility speaks also in Paul's other word, "By the grace of God, I am what I am."

❧❧❧

❖ Fourth Day, Eleventh Week

And it came to pass in these days, that he went out into the mountain to pray; and he continued all night in prayer to God.—*Luke 6: 12*

And at even, when the sun did set, they brought unto him all that were sick, and them that were possessed with demons. And all the city was gathered together at the door. And he healed many that were sick with divers diseases, and cast out many demons; and he suffered not the demons to speak, because they knew him.

And in the morning, a great while before day, he rose up and went out, and departed into a desert place, and there prayed.—*Mark 1: 32–35*

And straightway he constrained his disciples to enter into the boat, and to go before him unto the other side to Bethsaida, while he himself sendeth the multitude away. And after he had taken leave of them, he departed into the mountain to pray.—*Mark 6: 45, 46*

These are typical passages revealing the habit of the Master. He said himself that his work was done by the power of God's Spirit, and we see him here seeking in prayer fresh appropriations of strength for service. *Compare the self-sufficiency of your life, which always means shallowness and spiritual pride, with the dependence of the Master on the Father.* Recall Archbishop Trench's great sonnet:

Lord, what a change within us one short hour
    Spent in Thy presence will avail to make!

What heavy burdens from our bosoms take;
What parched grounds refresh, as with a shower?
We kneel, and all around us seems to lower;
    We rise, and all the distant and the near
    Stands forth in sunny outline, brave and clear!
We kneel, how weak! we rise, how full of power!

Why, therefore, should we do ourselves this wrong
Or others, that we are not always strong;
That we are ever overborne with care;
    That we should ever weak or heartless be,
Anxious or troubled, when with us is prayer,
    And joy and strength and courage are with Thee?

ॐॐॐ

❖ Fifth Day, Eleventh Week

Ask, and it shall be given you; seek, and ye shall find; knock, and it shall be opened unto you: for every one that asketh receiveth; and he that seeketh findeth; and to him that knocketh it shall be opened. Or what man is there of you, who, if his son shall ask of him a loaf, will give him a stone; or if he shall ask for a fish, will give him a serpent? If ye then, being evil, know how to give good gifts unto your children, how much more shall your Father who is in heaven give good things to them that ask him?—*Matt. 7: 7–11*

Some have wondered why we should pray, if God knows better what we need than we do, and is more than willing to bestow it. The answer is plain: God cannot crowd his real blessings on us unless we are open hearted toward them, any more than a father can crowd education on an unwilling boy. Reception of God's ideals for us, his will for our life, his power to endure and achieve, is vital work, and prayer is the best name for that kind of receptive labor. *God can do in and through a man who prays what he cannot do in and through a man who does not pray, just as a teacher can do for a boy who studies what he cannot do for a boy who refuses. Prayer is one form of cooperation with God, by which we give him the opportunity of doing in us what he has wanted to do, perhaps, for years.*

ॐॐॐ

Prayer is not primarily asking God to do special things for us; prayer is never expecting God to alter his plans to suit our whim; prayer at its deepest must always be the soul's endeavor to open the way for God to do his divine will.

❖ Sixth Day, Eleventh Week

But Peter said unto him, Although all shall be offended, yet will not I. And Jesus saith unto him, Verily I say unto thee, that thou to-day, even this night, before the cock crow twice, shalt deny me thrice. But he spake exceeding vehemently, If I must die with thee, I will not deny thee. And in like manner also said they all.

And they come unto a place which was named Gethsemane: and he saith unto his disciples, Sit ye here, while I pray. And he taketh with him Peter and James and John, and began to be greatly amazed, and sore troubled. And he saith unto them, My soul is exceeding sorrowful even unto death: abide ye here, and watch. And he went forward a little, and fell on the ground, and prayed that, if it were possible, the hour might pass away from him. And he said, Abba, Father, all things are possible unto thee; remove this cup from me: howbeit not what I will, but what thou wilt.—*Mark 14: 29–36*

Surely the Master never wanted to beg God to change his lot more than in this terrible hour. Yet note his prayer's conclusion: "Not what I will, but what thou wilt." Prayer is not primarily asking God to do special things for us; prayer is never expecting God to alter his plans to suit our whim; prayer at its deepest must always be the soul's endeavor to open the way for God to do his divine will. We do not try by prayer to "move the arm that moves the world," but rather so to enter into spiritual fellowship with God's purpose, that the arm that moves the world can move us. *Has prayer come to mean this deepest experience to you—an inner fellowship with him who is not far from any one of us, a sensitive, listening spirit to hear his voice, sincere desire never to hamper his purpose in our lives, so that however much we wish any special thing, our petition ends, like the Master's: "Not what I will but what thou wilt"?*

❧❧❧

❖ Seventh Day, Eleventh Week

Now the works of the flesh are manifest, which are these: fornication, uncleanness, lasciviousness, idolatry, sorcery, enmities, strife, jealousies, wrath; factions, divisions, parties, envyings, drunkenness, revellings, and such like; of which I forewarn you, even as I did forewarn you, that they who practise such things shall not inherit the kingdom of God. But the fruit of the Spirit is love, joy, peace, longsuffering, kindness, goodness, faithfulness, meekness, self-control; against such there is no law. And they that are of Christ Jesus have crucified the flesh with the passions and the lusts thereof.—*Galatians 5: 19–24*

Consider Paul's list of the fruits of the spirit as a study of the character of Jesus. Note that these virtues here mentioned are of a kind more easily felt than defined. They are not particular details of duty, they are a spiritual radiance that illumines all special deeds and puts quality into them. It was not what the Master *did* alone, but far more what the Master *was, shining through what he did, that is winning the world to him. The value of any deed lies in the quality of the man who does it. The great need of the world is for spiritual quality in men, for depth and altitude of soul, for wealth of inward life, out of which special deeds shall come like a brook from the mountains, with power.* This was the secret of the Master's influence, and the sources lie far back in his life of prayer and fellowship with God. Are you neglecting this inward spring of spiritual wealth and strength?

ର ର ର

Comment for the Week

The deepest levels of Jesus' character are not touched when we take his virtues one by one and study them. Like the facets of a diamond the separate qualities in the Master's life only reveal and transmit the radiance that shines out from within. No facet is a sufficient explanation of itself, and does not itself possess the source of its own lustre. Behind the splendor of the flashing surfaces is the quality of the diamond's heart, and while this facet or that may be partially described, who shall find words even to suggest that more subtle matter, the quality of light that illumines every separate surface and gives a common lustre to them all?

The spiritual quality of a man's goodness comes in part from the reasons why he is good.

Especially in the Master's character is it necessary to seek the value of his virtues in the spirit that irradiates them. His virtues are more than themselves; they are vehicles for a spiritual quality. No man ever drops his deeds like bare coins into the treasury of the world, each one stamped with a fixed value. Rather in passing from us into other lives our deeds carry something of ourselves along; they possess an atmosphere, a spiritual climate. A man contributes to his deeds a fragrance, good or ill, which they have gathered from his soul, and by which they are distinguished from the same deeds done by any other man. So the Master's spirit suffuses all the separate virtues he possesses, and all the deeds he does; they carry a glory not their own; they come like Moses with a shining face from out the communion of his heart with God. When he did so lowly a service as to gird himself with a towel and wash his disciples' feet, the deed, coming from him, carried a meaning, was luminous with a quality and a significance, which any one of us would try in vain to put into the same action. This is the innermost secret of the Master's character—his irradiating spirit, which gave the peculiar quality that we recognize in all his deeds.

Perhaps as direct a path as we can follow into the appreciation of this inner spirit of the Master is the study of his motives. All goodness is not alike, as all light is not alike; and the ascent from the whale-oil lamp of an Esquiniau [Eskimo] to the sunshine at noon, is not too violent a comparison to picture the ascending degrees of goodness in the human heart. Now this difference in the quality of goodness is in part a matter of motive. Motives do not merely support character, as foundations support a house; motives enter into the nature of character as springs contribute their quality to the streams that flow from them. The way by which a man comes into his goodness, the ideas which direct him, the motives which impel him, the considerations which sustain him, enter into the very texture of his character and determine its nature. *The spiritual quality of a man's goodness comes in part from the reasons why he is good.*

This community of spirit between the Master and his Father, this consciousness of God as the indwelling power of his life, the speaker of his words, the doer of his deeds, without whom he could do nothing and with whom he was at one, was to the disciples the preeminent impression of Jesus' personality.

When one considers the Master, for example, he sees clearly that the *fear of punishment cannot explain that kind of character.* Some men, with scrupulous prudence, keep the social conventionalities, as they observe the traffic regulations on a city street, because of natural and legal penalties associated with their violation. Between character so motived and the goodness of the Master, the difference is obvious. So we might range through the lower orders of virtue—goodness based on the recognition of the fact that "Honesty is the best policy," goodness based on the desire for a respected reputation—and we would find that the quality of the Master's character is too fine, its depth is too profound, to have sprung altogether from such considerations. He did not deny that the Pharisees had a kind of righteousness, but he saw that it was a poor kind: "Except your righteousness shall *exceed* the righteousness of the scribes and Pharisees," he said, "ye shall in no wise enter into the kingdom of heaven" (Matt. 5: 20).

Above all other reasons for the unique quality which characterized Jesus' goodness was his consciousness of fellowship with God. This was the master motive of his life. What John reports him to have cried in prayer,: O righteous Father, the world knew thee not, but I knew thee" (John 17: 25), Matthew remembers him saying to his disciples, "No one knoweth the Son, save the Father; neither doth any know the Father save the Son" (Matt. 11: 27). All his life is saturated with this consciousness of an incommunicable relationship with God, a unique union of life with the Divine. We are dealing here with the familiar idea of Jesus' oneness with God; only we are dealing with it not as a doctrine of the Church, but as an element in Jesus' own experience. This consciousness suffused his character and gave it quality; no virtue in his life escaped the hallowing influence of this filial fellowship with God.

This community of spirit between the Master and his Father, this consciousness of God as the indwelling power of his life, the speaker of his words, the doer of his deeds, without whom he could do nothing and with whom he was at one (John 5: 30; 14: 9, 10, 14), was to the disciples the preeminent impression of Jesus' personality. They knew and praised his various virtues, his love, forgiveness, righteousness, and patience; but like the sun in a system where moral excellencies are the planets, shine the words, "God was in Christ." To the disciples the outstanding fact about the manhood of the Master was that they could not dissociate him from God. His life always bore reference to the Divine, with whom he lived in filial communion and by whom he was empowered. But even this impression which Jesus made on those who knew him is not the heart of the matter; we must look to the inner spiritual life of the Master for that. *Before his oneness with the Father was either a doctrine, or an impression on his followers, it was an experience in him.* Let us say it reverently: in the mystical depths of his spirit he lived in perfect communion with God. To pick out special details of his life to show how close and unbroken this communion was is like taking special bucketfuls from the sea to prove that the sea is wet. But it is all wet: the essential nature of it is of this one, uniform quality. The spirit of the Master gets its uniqueness from this fact that he was everywhere God-conscious.

The Master prayed as naturally as a child breathes.

The Master's life of communion with the Father is evidenced in his way of thinking and speaking about God. Only a limited part of our thought of God has sprung from our own immediate experience of him, our communion with him in prayer, our consciousness of his voice in conscience and ideals; only a little has come through the experience of forgiveness and the practice of his presence. But in Jesus you find no borrowed thoughts of God. We clamber up to God; he starts with God as an immediate intuition. God never is in his thought as an hypothesis to explain the world, never is discovered as a conclusion at the end of an argument; God, in a word, is not so much with the Master an object of thought as the subject of inward experience. He leaves us no new argument for God save this; that he showed us a life lived in perfect communion with the Father; he argued for God as a bay might prove the presence of the sea by letting in the tides. "I am not alone, but I and the Father that sent me" (John 8: 16); "He that sent me is with me; he hath not left me alone" (John 8: 29); "I and the Father are one" (John 10: 30); "That they may all be one; even as thou, Father, art in me, and I in thee, that they also may be in us" (John 17: 21); these Johannine phrases only make explicit what the earlier biographies continually imply concerning the immediate and intimate consciousness of God which motived and glorified the Master's life.

I believe, the first test of a truly great man is his humility.
—John Ruskin

Especially in his prayer life was this community of spirit between Jesus and the Father manifested. The Master prayed as naturally as a child breathes. Sometimes he prayed in triumph as on the Mount of Transfiguration when as he prayed, "the fashion of his countenance was altered" (Luke 9: 29); sometimes he prayed in grief, as in the Garden of Gethsemane, of which it is written that "Being in an agony he prayed more earnestly; and his sweat became as it were great drops of blood" (Luke 22: 44). He spent whole nights in prayer, arose long before day to pray, or at the sunset hour withdrew alone to commune with God (Luke 6: 12; Mark 1: 35; Mark 6: 46, 47). He preceded the crises of his life and followed his hard and perplexing labors with prayer, and if the solitude of place was lacking, he could withdraw into the solitude of his own soul. "It came to pass, as he was praying apart," says Luke, "the disciples were with him" (Luke 9: 18). He was a soul so great in spiritual apprehension that our best adjectives pass rather for impertinence than praise, and yet his prayers are as simple as a child's. "Father, into thy hands I commend my spirit," is the trustful self-commitment which he makes even in the crucifixion's agony. Yet so impressive was it to hear him pray that one of his biographers, referring in parenthesis to a geographical locality, describes it by saying, "The place where they ate the bread, after the Lord had given thanks" (John 6: 23). Just one thing the disciples are reported to have asked the Master to teach them; they wanted him to teach them to pray. In his communion with God he was so immediately conscious that the Father knew what things he had need of before the prayer was offered (Matt. 6: 8); he was so sure that God was more willing to give good gifts unto his children than they were to receive (Matt. 7: 9–11); he was so truly what another has written of him, "One who absolutely trusted the Unseen, who had utter confidence that Love was at the heart of all things, utter confidence also in the Absolute Power of that Absolute Love and in the liberty of that Love to help him," that he prayed as naturally as the sun shines or as mothers love their children. *Prayer was the spontaneous expression of his community of life with God.*

Out of such a life no deed could come, no virtue could emerge that was not distinguished by the quality of its source. All the elements in the Master's goodness which we have studied, his joy, his fearlessness, his fortitude, his magnanimity, are separate as incandescent arcs are, but they all burn with the same fire. This explains why it is often possible to find bravery or sacrificial devotion in other lives than his, that seem to equal the same virtues in him; but it is never possible to find the same quality which suffuses his courage and makes his sacrificial devotion a symbol of the love of God. *No virtue in him was the whole of itself; his spirit was the rest of it.* The Master's preeminence comes not chiefly from his describable virtues, but from those deep sources of his life with God, out of which his virtues flowed, begotten not made, and fragrant, every one of them, with the quality of his perfect fellowship with the Father.

This could be illustrated in many ways, but we may note especially the quality of humility in the Master as manifestly the consequence of his life with God. It is only in the light of such an attitude on Jesus' part as John records, "I can of myself do nothing" (John 5: 30), that we can understand the seeming contradiction between Jesus' amazing claims for himself on the one side and on the other his teaching of humility, and the impression which be makes of being "meek and lowly in heart." Many of the Master's words do not at all have a humble note in them: "Heaven and earth shall pass away; but my words shall not pass away" (Mark 13: 31); "The Son of man shall come in his glory, and all the angels with him, then shall he sit on the throne of his glory: and before him shall be gathered all nations" (Matt. 25: 31); "He that loveth father or mother more than me is not worthy of me" (Matt. 10: 37); "He that denieth me in the presence of men shall be denied before the angels of God" (Luke 12: 9).

Such a spirit in Jesus is the only explanation of his absolute self-assurance on one side and his lowliness of heart upon the other. His power was not in him, but through him.

These expressions and others like them, culminating in his acceptance of the title of Messiah (Mark 8: 29), and his claim to be the only one who thoroughly knows God (Matt. 11: 27), appear at first sight to be violent contradictions of the spirit of humility. And yet he taught humility continually: "Blessed are the meek, for they shall inherit the earth" (Matt. 5: 5); "Whosoever therefore shall humble himself as this little child, the same is the greatest in the kingdom of heaven" (Matt. 18: 4); "Whosoever shall exalt himself shall be humbled; and whosoever shall humble himself shall be exalted" (Matt. 23: 12). To illustrate a truth so fundamental in his thought he told stories; one in praise of a guest who took a lowly seat rather than crowd into the more distinguished places (Luke 14: 7ff); another in praise of a publican who humbled himself before God (Luke 18: 12ff). And even stranger yet, this same person who made such amazing claims for himself, said also, "Why callest thou me good? none is good save one, even God" (Mark 10: 18); he spoke of himself as "meek and lowly" (Matt. 11: 29); and he made the impression of humility so distinctly on the first generation of Christians that among Paul's few words in description of the life and character of Jesus we find the phrase, "the meekness and gentleness of Christ" (II Cor. 10: 1).

Not from me but from above it all has come.—Haydn

The best explanation of this apparent contradiction was written by Mr. Ruskin, and has been well quoted in this connection in Dr. Speer's "The Man Christ Jesus."[1] "I believe," says Mr. Ruskin, "the first test of a truly great man is his humility. I do not mean by humility doubt of his own power, or hesitation in speaking his opinions; but a right understanding of the relation between what he can do and say, and the rest of the world's doings and sayings. All great men not only know their business, but usually know that they know it, and are not only right in their main opinions, but they usually know that they are right in them, only they do not think much of themselves on that account. Arnolfo knows that be can build a good dome at Florence; Albert Dürer writes calmly to one who has found fault with his work, 'It cannot be done better;' Sir Isaac Newton knows that he has worked out a problem or two that would have puzzled anybody else; only they do not expect their fellowmen therefore to fall down and worship them. They have a curious undersense of powerlessness, feeling that the power is not in them, but *through* them, that they could not do or be anything else than God made them, and they see something divine and God-made in every other man they meet, and are endlessly, foolishly, incredibly merciful."

Such a spirit in Jesus is the only explanation of his absolute self-assurance on one side and his lowliness of heart upon the other. His power was not in him, but through him. When John represents him as saying that he was not speaking his own words, or doing his own deeds, or using his own strength, and that when people believed on him, they did not believe on him, but on God who sent him (John 5: 30; 14: 10, 24, 44), he is putting into clear outline the same spirit which the Master shows in the earlier biographies. Jesus had lost himself in manifesting the life and purpose of

1. Editor: This may refer to Robert E. Speer (1867–1947) and his 1896 *Studies of the Man Christ Jesus*. Ruskin is probably John Ruskin (1819–1900), an English artist, poet and writer with a strong interest in religion.

God, and in so doing he grew amazingly sure of his message and his preeminence, and amazingly humble in the consciousness of mediatorship. When Haydn wrote "The Creation," he cried, "Not from me but from above it all has come; "when Amiel was in one of his most elevated moods, be wrote, "I realize with intensity that man in all that he does that is great and noble is only the organ of something or someone higher than himself; "and this same consciousness of being able to do nothing of himself was alike the cause of the Master's confident self-assurance and of his humility which even waved aside the ascription of "good Master."

This really humble spirit of our Lord, in which he lived at his best for the sake of men and looked upon all his words and works as the power of God using him in ministry, glorified the separate excellencies of his character. Like the sun breaking into the jewel-room of a king and setting every stone ablaze, breaking up the fountains of the beautiful deep in each diamond and sapphire, emerald and pearl, so this spirit of Jesus illumined with more than earthly radiance the virtues of his life. The imitation of his several qualities is quite in vain, save as we too enter into the secret sources of his spirit and have fulfilled in us the promise of the Gospel, "be perfect as your heavenly Father is perfect" (Matt. 5: 48).

అ అ అ

Notes

12

The Measure of the Fullness of Christ

This study of the balanced qualities in the Master's character could be extended almost without limit. We undertake to exalt the gentleness of Jesus to whom mothers brought their children that he might lay his hands on them and pray, and we are at once compelled to note his fiery indignation also as he drives the money-changers from the Temple.

Daily Readings

❖ First Day, Twelfth Week

And Jesus went with them. And when he was now not far from the house, the centurion sent friends to him, saying unto him, Lord, trouble not thyself; for I am not worthy that thou shouldest come under my roof: wherefore neither thought I myself worthy to come unto thee: but say the word, and my servant shall be healed. For I also am a man set under authority, having under myself soldiers: and I say to this one, Go, and he goeth; and to another, Come, and he cometh; and to my servant, Do this, and he doeth it. And when Jesus heard these things, he marvelled at him, and turned and said unto the multitude that followed him, I say unto you, I have not found so great faith, no, not in Israel.—*Luke 7: 6–9*

And it was now about the sixth hour, and a darkness came over the whole land until the ninth hour, the sun's light failing: and the veil of the temple was rent in the midst. And Jesus, crying with a loud voice, said, Father, into thy hands I commend my spirit: and having said this, he gave up the ghost. And when the centurion saw what was done, he glorified God, saying. Certainly this was a righteous man.—*Luke 23: 44–47*

We are going to note this week the impression which the Master made on very different kinds of people. The two centurions in these passages were attracted by his authoritative and powerful character, whether shown in his daily ministry or in the manner of his death. Recall also the soldiers, sent to arrest him, who returned, saying, "Never man spake like this man!" It is interesting to add the testimony of Napoleon, a man of the centurion type: "Alexander, Caesar, Charlemagne, and I have founded great empires, but upon what did these creations of our genius depend? Upon force! Jesus alone founded his empire upon love, and to this very day millions would die for him. I think I understand something of human nature, and I tell you that all these were men and I am a man. None else is like him. Jesus Christ was more than a man." *Consider the ways in which the Master appeals to all that is strongest and most military in you.*

ৡৡৡ

❖ Second Day, Twelfth Week

And they were bringing unto him little children, that he should touch them: and the disciples rebuked them. But when Jesus saw it, he was moved with indignation, and said unto them, Suffer the little children to come unto me; forbid them not; for to such belongeth the kingdom of God. Verily I say unto you, Whosoever shall not receive the kingdom of God as a little child, he shall in no wise enter therein. And he took them in his arms, and blessed them, laying his hands upon them.—*Mark 10: 13–16*

How deep the contrast between the centurions and the children, and yet how clearly there is, with the military quality in Jesus to which the first responded, the childlike quality also which drew the children! Think of what the coming of the Master has meant to childhood, of his birthday significantly interpreted as the children's festival, of the deepening estimation of children wherever the Gospel comes; and note that all this development has its legitimate source in the Master's personal attitude. *Consider the qualities in him that must have made children love him, and think over the many ways in which he appeals to you upon the side of your childlike qualities, sincerity, simplicity, humility and gentleness.*

ৡৡৡ

A Christianity which does not impel a man to save his fellows has but little that is akin to the spirit of Christ.—Quintin Hogg

❖ Third Day, Twelfth Week

And after these things he went forth, and beheld a publican, named Levi, sitting at the place of toll, and said unto him, Follow me. And he forsook all, and rose up and followed him.

And Levi made him a great feast in his house: and there was a great multitude of publicans and of others that were sitting at meat with them. And the Pharisees and their scribes murmured against his disciples, saying, Why do ye eat and drink with the publicans and sinners? And Jesus answering said unto them, They that are in health have no need of a physician; but they that are sick. I am not come to call the righteous but sinners to repentance.—*Luke 5: 27–32*

And walking by the sea of Galilee, he saw two brethren, Simon who is called Peter, and Andrew his brother, casting a net into the sea; for they were fishers. And he saith unto them, Come ye after me, and I will make you fishers of men. And they straightway left the nets, and followed him. And going on from thence he saw two other brethren, James the son of Zebedee, and John his brother, in the boat with Zebedee their father, mending their nets; and he called them. And they straightway left the boat and their father, and followed him.—*Matt. 4: 18–22*

These men were evidently prosperous business men, very different from children. Consider the qualities in the Master that made it possible for him to present his Cause to them in such a way that they counted it a privilege to devote their lives to him and his work. How often has the Master called to his service men of the type of the Sons of Zebedee, and persuaded them to harness their ability, and not seldom, their money into the work of the Kingdom! Quintin Hogg's biographer, speaking of Hogg's great service to the poor boys of London in the Polytechnic Institute which he founded,[1] says, "The Polytechnic had indeed become his sole purpose in life, his very reason for existence; his business never suffered, but outside that, his philanthropic work claimed his faculties and absorbed his thoughts until there was no room for any private considerations apart from it, any personal desires or ambitions that were not concerned with the perfecting and supporting of it." Said Quintin Hogg himself: "A Christianity which does not impel a man to save his fellows has but little that is akin to the spirit of Christ." *Have you let the Master take possession of your practical ability?*

❧❧❧

❖ Fourth Day, Twelfth Week

And it came to pass soon afterwards, that he went about through cities and villages, preaching and bringing the good tidings of the kingdom of God, and with him the twelve, and certain women who had been healed of evil spirits and infirmities: Mary that was called Magdalene, from whom seven demons had gone out, and Joanna the wife of Chuzas Herod's

---

1. Editor: Quintin Hogg (1845–1903) founded the Regent Street Polytechnic, one of many "ragged schools" and other programs (hostels, savings clubs, and recreational programs) that provided practical and religious training for poor children in England. The biography referred to may be *Quintin Hogg: A Biography* by Ethel M. Hogg, his daughter.

steward, and Suzanna, and many others, who ministered unto them of their substance.—*Luke 8: 1–3*

Now as they went on their way, he entered into a certain village: and a certain woman named Martha received him into her house. And she had a sister called Mary, who also sat at the Lord's feet, and heard his word. But Martha was cumbered about much serving; and she came up to him, and said, Lord, dost thou not care that my sister did leave me to serve alone? bid her therefore that she help me. But the Lord answered and said unto her, Martha, Martha, thou art anxious and troubled about many things: but one thing is needful: for Mary hath chosen the good part, which shall not be taken away from her.—*Luke 10: 38–42*

And many women were there beholding from afar, who had followed Jesus from Galilee, ministering unto him: among whom was Mary Magdalene, and Mary the mother of James and Joses, and the mother of the sons of Zebedee.—*Matt. 27: 55, 56*

The differences in the characteristic virtues of manhood and womanhood are proverbial; but the Master, even when living his homeless life on earth, made direct appeal not only to centurions and practical men, but to good women. Womanhood has a power of spiritual insight often denied to man, is sensitive to finer influences than manhood feels; and Browning expresses womanhood's eminence as the conservator of our spiritual ideals, when he says to his wife,

You must be just before, in fine,
    See, and make me see, for your part,
New depths of the divine.

This spiritual insight of womanhood has from the beginning appreciated in the Master qualities which men alone might have missed. The finest in womanhood, as well as in manhood, has looked to him for its ideal and has responded to his appeal for loyal devotion. *Think of those qualities which go to make the noblest womanhood and see how surely they are present in the manhood of the Master.*

᠅᠅᠅

❖ Fifth Day, Twelfth Week

And Jesus answering said unto him, Simon, I have somewhat to say unto thee. And he saith, Teacher, say on. A certain lender had two debtors: the one owed five hundred shillings, and the other fifty. When they had not wherewith to pay, he forgave them both. Which of them therefore will love him most? Simon answered and said, He, I suppose, to whom he forgave the most. And he said unto him, Thou hast rightly judged. And turning to the woman, he said unto Simon, Seest thou this woman? I entered into thy house, thou gavest me no water for my feet: but she hath wetted my feet with her tears, and wiped them with her hair. Thou gavest me no kiss: but she, since the time I came in, hath not ceased to kiss my feet. My head with oil thou didst not anoint: but she hath anointed my feet with ointment. Wherefore I say unto thee, Her sins, which are many, are forgiven; for she loved much: but to whom little is forgiven, the same loveth little. And he said unto her, Thy sins are forgiven.—*Luke 7: 40–48*

Read the story immediately preceding this passage. Here is a type of woman outlawed by good men and often especially despised by good women. What was it in the Master that brought her ashamed, penitent, aspiring, grateful, to his feet? Note that his was not goodness in a negative sense, but outgoing, sacrificial, saving goodness that encouraged the outcast with a new hope and made prodigals believe anew in spiritual possibilities for their own lives. How numberless are the men and women who have been drawn by the Master into a new life, that before had seemed beyond their reach! *Consider his appeal to you in any sin that has marred your life and perhaps has discouraged your will. Can you imagine for a moment his consenting to any dismal view of your case, if like this woman, you were truly penitent?*

❧❧❧

❖ Sixth Day, Twelfth Week

He said therefore to the multitudes that went out to be baptized of him. Ye offspring of vipers, who warned you to flee from the wrath to come? Bring forth therefore fruits worthy of repentance, and begin not to say within yourselves, We have Abraham to our father: for I say unto you, that God is able of these stones to raise up children unto Abraham. And even now the axe also lieth at the root of the trees: every tree therefore that bringeth not forth good fruit is hewn down, and cast into the fire.

And as the people were in expectation, and all men reasoned in their hearts concerning John, whether haply he were the Christ; John answered, saying unto them all, I indeed baptize you with water; but there cometh he that is mightier than I, the latchet of whose shoes I am not worthy to unloose: he shall baptize you in the Holy Spirit and in fire: whose fan is in his hand, thoroughly to cleanse his threshing-floor, and to gather the wheat into his garner; but the chaff he will burn up with unquenchable fire.—*Luke 3: 7–9; 15–17*

How different the personality of John the Baptist from those whom we have just considered, centurions, children, men of business, women, and penitent sinners! John is a fearless prophet of righteousness, blazing with condemnation of the people's sins. Read in Matthew 11: 7–19, the Master's appreciation of John, and note the rugged qualities which he admires in the Baptist—his austerity, his uncompromising firmness. Is it not difficult to imagine John affectionately blessing little children or appreciating the finer elements in womanhood? Yet Jesus who is as gentle as a child and has womanhood's sensitiveness, has also in his own life the qualities that draw the devout adoration of this austere, ascetic prophet. Moral vigor was John's specialty, and yet he says of the Master, "*Mightier* than I, the latchet of whose shoes I am not worthy to unloose." *Consider the amazing combination of contrasted qualities that go to make up the character of our Lord.*

҈҈҈

❖ Seventh Day, Twelfth Week

Now when morning was come, all the chief priests and the elders of the people took counsel against Jesus to put him to death: and they bound him, and led him away, and delivered him up to Pilate the governor.

Then Judas, who betrayed him, when he saw that he was condemned, repented himself, and brought back the thirty pieces of silver to the chief priests and elders, saying, I have sinned in that I betrayed innocent blood. But they said, What is that to us? see thou to it. And he cast down the pieces of silver into the sanctuary, and departed; and he went away and hanged himself.—*Matt. 27: 1–5*

Now all the publicans and sinners were drawing near unto him to hear him. And both the Pharisees and the scribes murmured, saying, This man receiveth sinners, and eateth with them.—*Luke 15: 1, 2*

Let these passages suggest the impression which Jesus made on those who were unfaithful or hostile to him. Think of the charges made against him by his enemies, that he was too progressive, supplanting old Jewish traditions with his spiritual Gospel, that he was too liberal, welcoming outcasts to his fellowship, that he was too kind, forgiving even gross sinners, if they were penitent. Recall Pilate insisting that he found no fault in him, and Judas shamed to suicide by his betrayal of the innocent. *The gospels are not made up of the adulations of Jesus' friends; they are largely concerned with the charges of Jesus' enemies. Can you think of a single charge that does not imply a virtue?* Here is a character, then, whose authoritative power attracted soldiers, whose gentleness drew children to him, whose spiritual quality won good women to his discipleship, whose hope-bringing mercy drew discouraged sinners to a new life, whose fearless advocacy of righteousness awakened the enthusiasm of a prophet; a character whose enemies, when they condemned him, condemned him for qualities that seem to us now his virtues.

Who that one moment has the least descried him,
    Dimly and faintly, hidden and afar,
Doth not despise all excellence beside him,
    Pleasures and powers that are not and that are?

&ro;&ro;&ro;

Alexander, Caesar, Charlemagne, and I have founded great empires, but upon what did these creations of our genius depend? Upon force! Jesus alone founded his empire upon love, and to this very day millions would die for him. I think I understand something of human nature, and I tell you that all these were men and I am a man. None else is like him. Jesus Christ was more than a man.—Napoleon

---

Comment for the Week

In the course of our studies on the character of Jesus, we have been compelled continually to notice the remarkable poise in which the Master holds opposing virtues that with us are most difficult of combination. No sooner have we emphasized one quality in him, such as his amazing self-assurance, than we must balance our thought by laying stress upon the contrasting quality, his profound humility. We have noted his severity in moral standards and his sternness in judgment coupled with an unfailing appreciation of even faint beginnings of genuine goodness in any man; we have noted his intense susceptibility to sorrow, his heart quick as the apple of an eye to feel the hurt of others' misery and of his own, but yet joined with it his exhaustless cheer and joy; we have noted his combination of ambition, that included God's eternal purpose for the world, with devoted interest in apparently insignificant persons. This spherical balance in the Master's character has always attracted the attention of those who studied him. The difficulty of attaining such a poise between contrasted virtues has been elaborated by Dr. Bushnell[2] in a passage long since become classic: "Men undertake to be spiritual, and they become ascetic; or, endeavoring to hold a liberal view of the comforts and pleasures of society, they are soon buried in the world, and slaves to its fashions; or, holding a scrupulous watch to keep out every particular sin, they become legal, and fall out of liberty; or, charmed with the noble and heavenly liberty, they run to negligence and irresponsible living; so the earnest become violent, the fervent fanatical and censorious, the gentle waver, the firm turn bigots, the

2. Editor: This should be Horace Bushnell (1802–76), a Congregational pastor in Hartford, Connecticut who was one of the leading theologians in nineteenth-century America. His books include: *Christian Nurture, God in Christ* and *Christ in Theology.* He was also responsible for Hartford creating the nation's first public park.

liberal grow lax, the benevolent ostentatious. Poor human infirmity can hold nothing steady. Where the pivot of righteousness is broken, the scales must needs slide off their balance." In our concluding study, therefore, we may well note at greater length the remarkable poise and completeness of the Master's character, the evidences of which have so continually forced themselves on our attention.

Perhaps no two ideals are more difficult to hold in balance than self-culture and self-denial. The one is represented by Goethe in a letter to Lavater: "The desire to raise the pyramid of my existence, the base of which is laid already, as high as possible into the air absorbs every other desire, and scarcely ever quits me;" the other is represented in a saying of Thomas a Kempis: "What is the reason why some of the saints were so perfect and contemplative? Because they labored to mortify themselves wholly to all earthly desires; and therefore they could with their whole heart fix themselves on God." On the one side are the virtues of culture, refinement, self-realization; on the other the virtues of self-abnegation, self-effacement and self-sacrifice. Now it is plain that the Master recognized the necessity of both of these ideals. When he said "Love thy neighbor as thyself" (Matt. 19: 19), he commanded us to love ourselves well and then love others just as much. When he said, "All things therefore whatsoever ye would that men should do unto you, even so do ye also unto them" (Matt. 7: 12), he commanded us to desire the best for ourselves and then seek the same for others. But this just balance between desire for self and devotion to others has been the most difficult problem in character. How did the Master solve the dilemma?

The secret of the inclusive balance of Jesus' life in regard to self-culture and self-denial is suggested in John's gospel, where in the Master's prayer at the last supper, he said, "For their sakes, I sanctify myself" (John 17: 19). That is, instead of choosing, like Goethe, one set of the contrasted virtues, or, like a mediaeval anchorite, the other, he combined them in the unity of a life, lived at its noblest and best, for the sake of others. He fed himself on the best reading of his time, the prophets of the Old Testament, and he sought spiritual insight into the beauty and significance of nature, that he himself might have a richer life with which to serve the world; he purified his spirit in prayer, like water running through the sun, that he might be of largest serviceableness to his followers. *He saw that his friends, that the world, needed him at his best and that therefore self-realization and service are two sides of the same thing.* He saw that human hearts are built in suites, like rooms, open to each other, but that sometimes only one room in the series opens to the outer air of God; so that whatever of the divine life reaches the others must first of all come through that one room. Jesus, therefore, overcame temptation and steadied himself in prayer and refreshed his soul from every spiritual reservoir within his reach, not for his own sake only, but for his friends' sake, that through the enrichment of his life they might be enriched. This sort of prayer he illustrated in his parable where a man with a bare cupboard has a friend come to visit him, and feeling the shame of having so little to offer, the host goes to his rich neighbor, saying, "Lend me three loaves, for a friend of mine is come to me from a journey and I have nothing to set before him" (Luke 11: 5, 6). That is Jesus' type of prayer. He sought a rich life for the sake of those who came to him for help; for their sake, he sanctified himself. When he sought the life in which his own self rose "as high as possible into the air," he found that life by losing himself in service for others (Matt. 10: 39). To him, therefore, self-realization and self-denial were not separable and alien; they were two aspects of the same attitude toward men; they were held by him in the unity of a perfect balance.

We may note further that enthusiastic devotion to a cause is most difficult of combination with patience and freedom from anxiety. That both enthusiasm and patience were commended in the Master's teaching is clear to any one who even casually has read the gospels. The disciples were to be so devoted to the Kingdom that having put their hands to the plough, they would not even look back (Luke 9: 62), and yet they were not to be impatient when the Kingdom delayed its coming (Mark 4: 26ff), nor disquieted when they were persecuted (Matt. 15: 12, 13), nor anxious when the devil sowed tares among the wheat (Matt. 13: 25ff). It is easy for a man to be patient at the delay and seeming failure of a cause in which his interest is small and lax, but to be willing to forsake family and property for a cause, and still without anxious solicitude to watch its laggard progress and sometimes to see its imminent defeat, requires an amazing balance of character.

The gospels bear us evidence that the Master preserved that balance perfectly. His devotion was passionate, and Dr. Seeley[3] is right in saying: *"All other faults or deficiencies he could tolerate, but he could have neither part nor lot with men destitute of enthusiasm."* He thought it a bad, almost a fatal sign, in one who proposed to become a disciple, that he asked leave first to bid farewell to his relations (Luke 9: 61, 62). Another asked permission to bury his father, and was advised to let the dead—that is, those whose hearts were not animated by any strong passion or impulse— bury their dead (Luke 9: 59, 60). And once when it seemed that the magic of his presence and words would draw his entire audience into the number

---

3. Editor: This is probably John Robert Seeley (1834–95), a Latin professor at University College, London. He was known for stressing enthusiasm over the content of faith and for assuming (as many then did) that Christian ethics could be maintained without theology. Among his writings is *Ecce Homo: A Survey of the Life & Work of Jesus Christ* (1866).

of his followers, alarmed lest he should find himself surrounded by half-hearted or superficial and merely excitable adherents, he turned suddenly upon the crowd, and with one of those startling expressions which he seldom, and yet like all great reformers sometimes, employed, declared that he could receive no man who did not hate his father and mother and his own life (Luke 14: 26).

With all this enthusiasm, however, he yet patiently compared the processes of the Kingdom to the procedure of nature in bringing forth "first the blade, then the ear, then the full grain in the ear" (Mark 4: 28ff); he was sure that like a mustard seed the small beginnings of the Kingdom would issue in a triumphant result (Matt. 13: 31, 32); and that the little leaven of the Gospel would leaven the whole lump (Matt. 13: 33). He was not disconcerted by opposition into doubt of the issue of his Cause (Matt. 5: 12–14); he revealed in his life of trust in God the same spirit of freedom from anxious foreboding which his Sermon on the Mount commends (Matt. 6: 25ff); and perhaps most amazing fact of all, about to be crucified as a felon, he took pains to symbolize his death with broken bread and poured wine, in confident certainty of coming victory (Mark 14: 22). When Charles Lamb writes of his grandmother,

> For she had studied patience in the school of Christ;
> Much comfort she had thence derived
> And was a follower of the Nazarene,

we often are not sufficiently impressed by the marvel of the fact, that this teacher of patience to aged and humble people was a young enthusiast, burning with patriotism for a great Cause, ready to die for it and involve his followers in his sacrifice, but, in strange conjunction with this ardent passion, was unanxious in his thought of tomorrow and sublimely patient in his work and his endurance.

This study of the balanced qualities in the Master's character could be extended almost without limit. We undertake to exalt the gentleness of Jesus to whom mothers brought their children that he might lay his hands on them and pray, and we are at once compelled to note his fiery indignation also as he drives the money-changers from the Temple. We undertake an appreciation of the liberality of Jesus, who broke down racial and sectarian boundaries in his sympathy, and extended welcome to the Gentiles, and we are compelled to stress, upon the other side, the strictness of Jesus who would not abate for compassion's sake one least emphasis upon the requirements of righteousness, and who said, "Narrow is the gate, and straitened the way that leadeth unto life, and few are they that find it" (Matt. 7: 14). But perhaps the most illuminating way in which we may perceive the completeness of the Master's character is to note the universality of his appeal, the manner in which his character has overpassed and comprehended all the deep divisions of our human life.[4]

There, for example, is the division between successive generations of men. When Mark Twain wrote his *Connecticut Yankee at King Arthur's Court,* he put his finger for purposes of humor on the ridiculous incongruities that are sure to arise when a man of one century imagines himself as living in another. The differences between the successive generations are profound and radical. If a man had knowledge and imagination enough to see in panorama the changes since Jesus was on earth; if he could not only watch the outward events of passing dynasties and fortunes in war, but could enter into the thoughts of each new century as it came, its social ideals, its scientific conclusions, its political beliefs, its philosophies and theologies, what bewildering, kaleidoscopic changes would pass before him! All the difference between autocracy and democracy, between a flat earth under the upturned bowl of the sky and the new universe of unimaginable distances, between miracles and regular law, between Greek metaphysics and the new philosophies would be there. And yet the Master outspans all the changes, and more people in the twentieth century take him for the Ideal than had ever heard of him in the first century or the tenth.

In minor ways, of course, the imitation of him is today impossible. His clothes, his Aramaic dialect, such things as these, and others deeper still in which his modes of thought and speech were necessarily conformed to the customs of his country and time, we cannot follow. But his *character* is so universal that even Renan cries, "Whatever the surprises of history, Jesus will never be surpassed." Men of all generations find in his trust in God, his loyalty to his Cause, his love of men, his quenchless hope, in these timeless and universal qualities suffused by his divine Spirit, their unsurpassable and complete Ideal. The characteristic virtue of some generations has been obedience to authority, and they saw the Master who said, "Thy will not mine be done;" the characteristic virtue of others has been revolt against false authority, and they saw the Master who said, "Ye make void the word of God by your tradition" (Mark 7: 13). The outstanding quality of some centuries was an ascetic subdual of the flesh, and theirs was the Master who said, "There are eunuchs, that made themselves eunuchs for the kingdom of heaven's sake" (Matt. 19: 12); and the outstanding quality of other centuries was joy in the beauties of this life, and theirs was the Master who exclaimed, "Even Solomon in all his glory was not arrayed like one of these" (Matt. 6: 29). If the emphasis of the time was upon the salvation of individual men, there was Jesus who said, "It is not the will of your Father that one of these little ones should perish" (Matt. 18: 14); and if the

4. Compare *The Universality of Jesus,* G. A. Johnston Ross.

emphasis was on the salvation of society, there was the Jesus who prayed, "Thy kingdom come, thy will be done on earth as it is in heaven." Each generation has been partial in its virtue, as each man is; the competing qualities, running to exaggeration, have reacted to their opposites, but in Jesus they are poised and balanced. And when you remember that this complete character came out of first century Palestine, provincial, exclusive, sectarian, how do you estimate him, holding sixty generations in his spiritual mastership, and making men of twenty centuries feel that when they tried to comprehend him, they were trying to mete out heaven with a span?

Again, this universal appeal of Jesus has overleaped the deep divisions of one race from another. Rudyard Kipling knows both Orient and Occident; he is at home alike in England, India or the United States; and his verdict is,

Oh East is East, and West is West, and never the twain shall meet.

But the twain have met. What is there most significantly Oriental that is not in Jesus? Does the Indian at his best feel, as we never do, the futility of this present life and the supremacy of the spirit? So the Master says, "What shall it profit a man if he gain the whole world?" Does the Indian at his best feel, as we never do, that the completion of religious experience is perfect communion with the Absolute Being? So the glory of the Master's life was community of soul with God. Does the Indian love, as we seldom do, the life of quiet prayer and contemplation? So Jesus sent multitudes away that he might preserve unspoiled his hours of solitary prayer (Matt. 14: 23). Then Jesus is an Oriental; his life is fitted to the mystical and contemplative East! But the same Jesus who was as contemplative as an Oriental said: "Not every one that saith unto me, Lord, Lord, but he that *doeth the will* of my Father" (Matt. 7: 21); "Everyone that heareth these words of mine, and *doeth them,* shall be likened unto a wise man, who built his house upon the rock" (Matt. 7: 24); "Whosoever shall *do the will* of my Father, he is my brother, and sister, and mother" (Matt. 12: 50); "I must *work the works* of him that sent me while it is day" (John 9: 4). The Orient has become so contemplative that it has forgotten deeds; the Occident has become so practical that it has forgotten contemplation: but in Jesus the best virtues of both are present in a perfect balance. He is the poised fulfilment of the excellencies of all tongues and tribes and peoples and nations. As a Brahman exclaimed when he first heard the story of Jesus, "O Christ, thou art the only Buddha!"

We may note still further the way the ideal of character in Jesus overleaps the deep division between manhood and womanhood. The two sexes represent two spheres of character; they move in two realms of temperament; the glory of their life together has never been in identity of function but in balanced harmony. *Yet we take it for granted that both should find their ideal in Christ.* Wherever men live by themselves apart from the civilizing influence of woman, their strength runs to roughness, their independent will to rudeness and vulgarity; wherever women live by themselves apart from the tonic, military attitude of man, their idealism runs to sentiment and their powers of loyalty lose their temper. The two need each other for completion:

> The man be more of woman, she of man;
> He gain in sweetness and in moral height,
> Nor lose the wrestling thews that throw the world;
> She mental breadth, nor fail in childward care,
> Nor lose the childlike in the larger mind;
> Till at the last she set herself to man
> Like perfect music unto noble words.

This is the ideal, but where can we find the realization of this balanced harmony of qualities? Surely Christendom has not simply imagined it but has found it in the Master who combined the idealism, the tenderness, the capacity for loyalty and devotion which make womanhood beautiful, with the heroism, the undiscourageable will, the masterful leadership which are manhood's glory. Does a woman's heart turn toward children like a compass needle toward the pole? Yet when has a woman said, "Suffer little children to come unto me, and forbid them not," with more tenderness and grace than he? Does a man's heart turn toward a courageous fight with instinctive desire? Yet where is the man who has withstood his enemies more heroically than the Master did, until when they triumphed over his body, they had so little overcome his soul that he cried, "Weep not for me, but weep for yourselves!" (Luke 23: 28). Has a woman powers of devotion inconceivable to man? So Jesus having loved his own loved them unto the end. Does a man rejoice in powers of leadership? So Jesus said, "One is your teacher, and all ye are brethren" (Matt. 23: 8). In him the virtues of loyalty and endurance in which womanhood excels are singularly poised with the virtues of achievement which are manhood's crown; in him, as Paul put it, "There is neither male nor female."

The two sexes represent two spheres of character; they move in two realms of temperament; the glory of their life together has never been in identity of function but in balanced harmony.

We may note further the appeal of the Master's character to the successive stages in any individual's growth from childhood to old age. Youth, maturity, age—what unlike virtues they exhibit and what various

needs they bear! Childhood wants gentleness and friendly care; youth
wants leadership calling to knightly adventure; maturity wants wisdom and
steadying power in the midst of life's battle; old age wants constancy,
patience and the grace of fortitude. Yet all these various qualities which are
the characteristic virtues of the individual as he grows in years, and
achieves the graces that meet the need of his successive stages in
development, we find in Christ. Childhood is gentle but not strong; youth is
adventurous but not patient; maturity is courageous but often disillusioned
and cynical; old age is patient but often hopeless: but to an extent that
seems impossible in a character, whose years on earth numbered not more
than thirty-three, the Master comprehended in himself the virtues of all
ages without their defects—gentle and strong, adventurous and patient,
courageous and joyful, enduring and hopeful. The number of a person's
years has never changed the adequacy of Christ as the Ideal. The children
sing, "What a friend we have in Jesus!" youth sings, "The Son of God goes
forth to war!" the mature sing, "How firm a foundation, ye saints of the
Lord!" the aged sing,

> While life's dark maze I tread,
> And griefs around me spread,
>   Be thou my guide!

*All centuries, all races, both sexes, all ages find in the Master their
virtues consummated.* The white light in him gathers up all the split and
partial colors of our little spectrums. As we consider the significance of
this, his word possesses a fresh and persuasive meaning when he says, "Ye
call me Teacher and Lord, and ye do well, for so I am."

পপপ

Notes

Printed in the United Kingdom
by Lightning Source UK Ltd.
93305